FORBIDDEN HISTORY
HIDDEN ORDERS

The Secret Societies, Occult Rituals, and Shadow
Networks Shaping Human Destiny

ZACK D. HISTORY

FORBIDDEN HISTORY

Table of Contents

Introduction

Behind the Veil of Power

What if the greatest events in human history weren't decided on battlefields or in parliaments, but in candlelit chambers—by people who swore never to speak of what they planned? What if the coronations, coups, treaties, and "inevitable" crises we learn about in school are the surface ripples of deeper currents—rituals, oaths, symbols, and networks that move power quietly, deliberately, and often invisibly?

You already know some of the names whispered at the edges of that story: Templars, Freemasons, Rosicrucians, the Illuminati, Skull and Bones. But this book doesn't traffic in recycled legends or the same handful of claims you've heard a thousand times. Our aim is more ambitious: to map the durable architecture of secrecy itself—how it organizes people, how it transmits power across centuries, and how its rituals shape decisions that appear, to the uninitiated, as accidents or "the way things always go."

We will follow the trail from desert shrines and mystery rites to private banks and glass-walled boardrooms; from monastic archives to off-the-books airfields; from antiquity's guarded sanctuaries to today's invitation-only conclaves. The point is not to replace one official story

If history has two versions—the one taught to the masses and the one whispered in the corridors of hidden orders—this book is written to help you hear the second without losing your footing in the first.

with an extravagant counter-myth. It is to learn how to read power in two layers at once: the loud theater and the quiet choreography.

What Are "Hidden Orders"?

Let's define the term carefully. A hidden order is not merely a secret club, nor is it every private association with colorful regalia. A hidden order is a network of people who coordinate influence—religious, political, financial, cultural, or occult—by combining three elements: secrecy, ritual, and continuity.

- **Secrecy** is not just silence. It is a technology: the ability to move unseen; to compartmentalize information; to test loyalty; to encode meaning in symbols, architecture, and ranks; to plan without press or oversight; to transmit directives orally or through private channels.

- **Ritual** stabilizes identity across time. It binds the initiate to the group through repeated acts—oaths, ordeals, symbolic deaths and rebirths, pilgrimages, handshakes, passwords, calendars, and feast days—which make belonging visceral rather than merely rational.

- **Continuity** is the transmission of patterns—symbols, genealogies, endowments, archives—so that a network can lie dormant, reappear under another name, or repurpose itself to new regimes while retaining a recognizable ethos.

Hidden orders may be devout or cynical, idealistic or predatory. Some shelter endangered ideas, steward sacred objects, or protect dissent. Others exist to launder reputations, trade favors, or centralize power out of sight. But in every case, secrecy is not incidental; it is the operating system.

ANATOMY OF
A HIDDEN ORDER

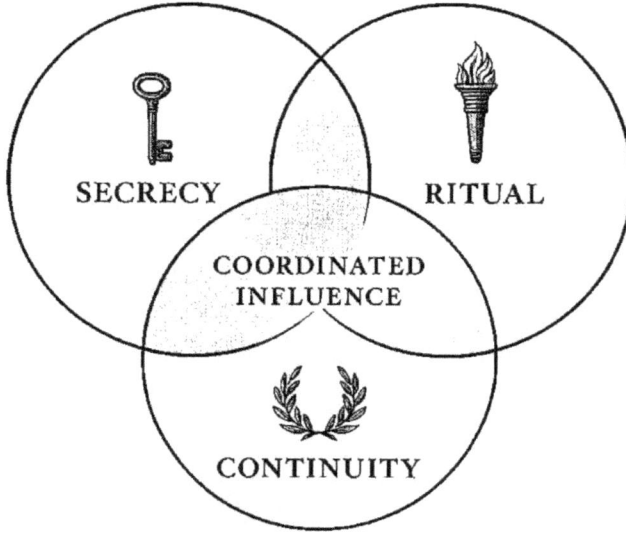

Why Don't We Hear the Whole Story?

You've likely noticed an odd pattern: textbook history foregrounds constitutions, elections, declarations, public speeches; it downplays closed retreats, private trusts, monastic scriptoria, or the role of initiation in making elites legible to one another. That is not an accident. Three forces obscure the study of hidden orders.

Suppression. Institutions that benefit from secrecy tend to write, fund, and preserve the records we inherit. Official narratives prefer "lone actors," "market forces," or "public interest" to low-visibility coordination. This is not always malicious—bureaucracies simply do not have fields in their forms for oaths, vows, or hand signals. What cannot be logged is presumed irrelevant.

Disinformation. The marketplace of myths is noisy. For every real archive, there is a carefully planted red herring; for every sober link between orders, there is a baroque fiction that makes the entire subject ridiculous by association. Wild claims have a purpose: they inoculate the public against looking closely at the plausible.

Fear of Exposure. Networks that thrive in quiet adapt quickly. When one set of rituals is scrutinized, forms shift. Names change. Front organizations flower. Houses are cleaned. Meeting places move. In an age of instantaneous leaks, the most resilient orders have learned to communicate in ways that leave minimal forensic traces.

THE THREE SCREENS

Screen 1: *Sanitization—powerful groups author the curricula and edit out ritual and secrecy.*
Screen 2: *Noise—a fog of fantasies hides credible patterns in plain sight.*
Screen 3: *Evasion—the networks themselves evolve faster than journalists can map them.*

Our Method: Connecting Myth, Evidence, and Suppressed Archives

This book navigates between credulity and cynicism by triangulating three kinds of sources:

1. **Myth:** stories, symbols, and rituals—how groups explain themselves, what they conceal in metaphor, what they replay in ceremony. Myths preserve memory under censorship; they also exaggerate. We treat them as artifacts—not as proof, but as maps that hint at buried paths.

2. **Evidence:** charters, minutes, financial ledgers, architectural programs, seals, genealogies, treaty drafts, meeting rosters, travel itineraries, and private correspondences. Where paper survives, we read against the grain, asking not just *what is said* but *who says it, to whom, and why now.*

3. **Suppressed & Obscure Archives:** misfiled boxes, defunct journals, out-of-print pamphlets, private collections, restricted repositories, and the gray literature around sanctuaries, orders, and discreet institutions. These do not automatically reveal "bombshells," but they often expose continuities of symbol and patronage that popular histories miss.

We will apply a repeatable protocol:

- **Symbolic Cross-Checks:** When the same emblem (say, the double-headed eagle or the beehive) recurs across institutions and centuries, we trace its migration: where it appears, who funds the structure carrying it, which families sponsor the work, which ceremonies attach to it.

- **Spatial Analysis:** Architecture is a memory palace. We read floor plans, sightlines, thresholds, and axial alignments: how temples, lodges, chapels, and clubhouses choreograph entry, advance, and exclusion; where sentinel rooms obstruct; where sancta sanctorum forbid the uninitiated.

- **Ritual Calendars:** We plot dates of meetings against religious feasts, solstices, and political anniversaries. Patterns of timing are messages.

- **Economic Footprints:** Follow the money, yes—but also follow the endowments and the lawyers. Private trusts, tax exemptions, discreet bankers, and real-estate shells are the ligaments of continuity.

- **Language Games:** Oaths and mottos are not ornaments. They transmit ethics and encode permissions. We read them in the original where possible and note shifts in translation that soften meaning for public ears.

HOW TO READ THIS BOOK

Rule 1: Ask what ritual achieves that an email cannot.
Rule 2: Track symbols across stone, paper, and seal.
Rule 3: Where a door is guarded, assume a memory is inside.
Rule 4: Distinguish secrecy as shelter (for faith, dissent, or conscience) from secrecy as leverage (for patronage, control, or extraction).

The Research Triangle

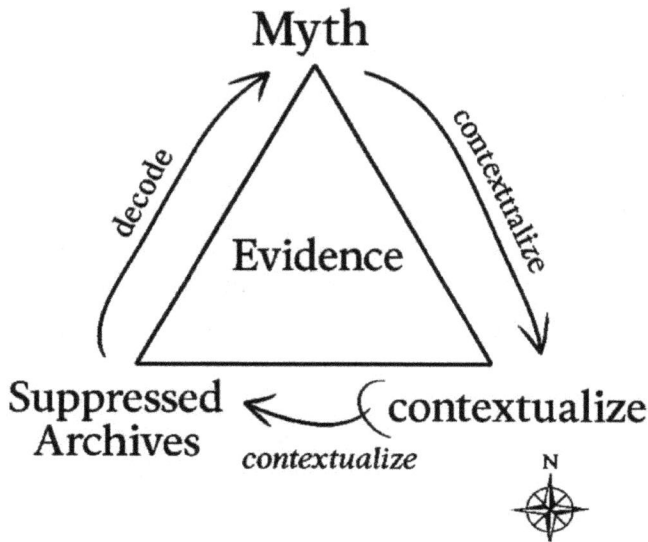

Myth

Evidence

decode

contextualize

Suppressed Archives

contextualize

contextualize

N

You, the Seeker

From this page forward, you are not a spectator. You are an initiate of the method. You will not be asked to accept a single sweeping theory; you will be asked to develop a habit of noticing what is staged and what is staged-for; of feeling where the architecture directs the body and where ritual directs the mind; of hearing power in its quieter registers.

We will walk together into spaces few see whole: desert monasteries whose libraries survived fires and inquisitions; chapels where relics and regalia re-enchant authority; vaults where dynastic wealth learned to vanish in plain sight; rural retreats where policy drafts were read aloud before they were ever printed. We will sit, figuratively, in the back benches of closed ceremonies and listen for the instructions that do not appear in the press release.

Skepticism is welcome here, but it must be skilled. The skeptic who dismisses ritual as mere costume will miss how belonging is manufactured. The believer who swallows every dramatic claim will miss how disinformation is manufactured. Between those extremes is a disciplined curiosity—the disposition of the seeker.

THE SEEKER'S PLEDGE

I will neither worship nor jeer at secrecy; I will study it. I will test claims, follow patterns, and revise my map when the evidence moves.

Why Humanity Is Obsessed with Secret Orders

The appetite for hidden orders is older than empire and wider than any one civilization. Children play at hide-and-seek; adolescents invent clubs; adults graduate to guilds, fraternities, and cabals. Why?

Shelter. When dominant powers surveil, people shelter the sacred, the vulnerable, and the unorthodox. Secrecy becomes a survival craft: passwords protect dissidents; underground rites preserve banned knowledge; cloisters shield fragile inheritances until the world is safer.

Belonging. Ritual intensifies solidarity. Nearly everyone hungers for rites that admit them, test them, transform them. In a fragmented world, orders offer continuity: a calendar, a language, a brotherhood or sisterhood with duties and gifts.

Leverage. Secrecy multiplies influence. It enables coordination without rebuttal, planning without delay, and alliance without public cost. Hidden orders can be the conscience of a culture—or its shadow government.

Aesthetics of Mystery. Humans are symbol-making creatures. We are drawn to thresholds, candles, vows, keys, veils, passwords, not just for utility but for beauty. Drama, pageantry, and architecture set the stage for moral imagination—or for manipulation.

These motives are double-edged. The same cloister that preserves a persecuted liturgy can also shield abuse. The same fraternity that nurtures friendship can ossify into nepotism. The same ritual that brings meaning can be exploited to dull conscience. Hence, the need for a method that discriminates shelter from leverage, stewardship from capture.

Veil Between Preservation and Influence

How Secrecy Has Shaped History More Than Open Politics

Open politics is the theater of legitimacy. Secrecy is the workshop where legitimacy is designed. Constitutions matter; so do committees that decide who interprets them. Elections matter; so do donor dinners that vet candidates years earlier. Revolutions matter; so do the lodges, cells, circles, monasteries, clubs, and retreats that incubate their ideas and coordinate their timing.

Consider five recurrent patterns:

1. **The Initiatory Ladder.** Orders do not simply recruit; they *form*. Degrees, stations, and ordeals create an escalator of loyalty. The person who ascends is not the person who entered.

Political life then borrows that escalator—placing initiates at chokepoints where symbolic capital is traded for office.

2. **The Seal and the Stone.** Architecture is not decor; it is instruction. Buildings encode hierarchies and memories. Capitals and capitals (pillars and cities) mirror one another: sacred axes align with secular avenues; reliquaries rhyme with vaults; chapels whisper to chambers of commerce.

3. **The Calendar and the Clock.** Timing is telling. Key decisions cluster around ritual dates—feasts, solstices, anniversaries—when networks are already gathered and moods are ripe. The "surprise" announcement often has an obvious ritual logic once you know the calendar.

4. **Sanctuary and Shadow.** Sanctuaries are designed to keep sacred things in and profane forces out. Their shadow in modern life is the secure compound: the retreat center, the cabinet room, the offsite bunker. Both organize attention; both edit who speaks; both create frames that make some options seem "unthinkable" and others "inevitable."

5. **Symbolic Continuities.** Power reuses signs because signs reuse power. A symbol confers custody: the one who bears the key, the sword, the seal, the lamp, the double-eagle, the eight-pointed star, the beehive, the laurel wreath, signals both inheritance and program. Follow the symbols across centuries, and patterns of patronage and policy emerge.

The point is not that "everything is a conspiracy." The point is that **power prefers form**—and the forms that preserve it best are those that can hide in ritual and stone.

The Journey Ahead

You're not reading a catalogue of curiosities. You're entering a guided investigation with five movements, each tuned to a different register of secrecy.

Part I—Ancient Orders: We begin with priesthoods, mystery schools, and temple economies. We will read the choreography of sanctuaries and the logic of initiations. Expect to encounter human beings who used rites to unite the visible and invisible—and institutions that learned to harness that union for governance.

Part II—Medieval Networks: Crusading orders, esoteric fellowships, and the birth of guild-based secrecy reshape Europe. Charters, seals, and patronage lines matter here. We will see how sacred vows translated into landholdings, courts of honor, and a legal personality that could outlive kings.

Part III—Modern Occult and Political Orders: As the old world cracks, initiatory groups migrate into salons, lodges, learned societies, and early national assemblies. Some nurture scientific inquiry and reform; others orchestrate the unadvertised side of revolution and reaction alike.

Part IV—Today's Shadow Networks: We explore the places where modern elites still retreat—private banks, monastic repositories, conclaves, fraternities, and "closed-door" meetings with no minutes. We will not guess wildly; we will map patterns: symbols, calendars, patronage, and agendas that recur.

Part V—The Codebook of Symbols, Rituals, and Influence: Here you receive the reader's Rosetta: a field guide to decoding emblems, floor plans, liturgies of belonging, and the habitus of hidden power. The aim is not to make you paranoid; it is to make you literate.

Workbook Bonus: Scattered through these chapters are exercises: match a building's plan to its ritual needs; trace a symbol's migration; annotate a timeline; test a headline against a calendar of feasts and anniversaries; draft your own side-by-side reading of public and private versions of an event. You will not just read a map—you will learn to draw one.

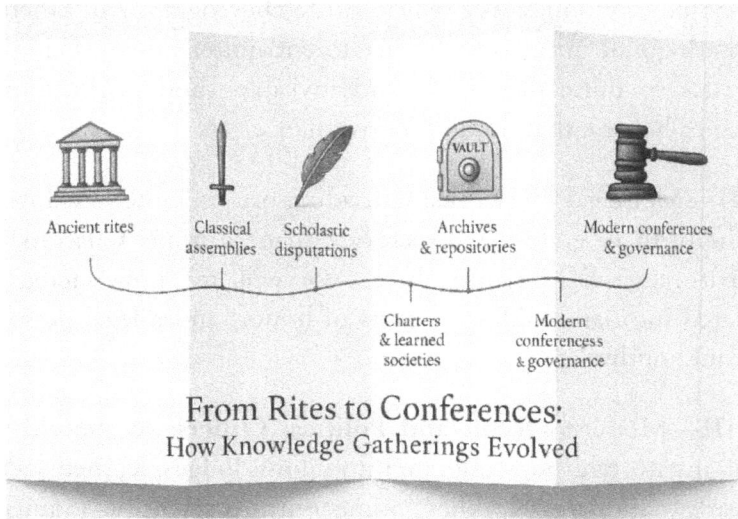

| Ancient rites | Classical assemblies | Scholastic disputations | Archives & repositories | Modern conferences & governance |

Charters & learned societies

Modern conferencess & governance

From Rites to Conferences:
How Knowledge Gatherings Evolved

Raising the Stakes

Why does any of this matter now? Because the tug-of-war between publicity and secrecy is accelerating, not resolving. Digital life has made some secrets harder to keep and others easier to hide. Algorithms profile publics at scale; encrypted channels shelter private directives; the theater of openness—press conferences, threaded posts, livestreamed hearings—creates the impression that everything important is on stage. Meanwhile, the quiet arts of coordination persist.

Three reasons to keep going:

1. Democratic Realism. If we want a credible civic life, we must learn to see how decisions are *prepared*. Modern polities are ruled not only by law and vote, but by norms shaped in spaces free from electoral accountability. That does not automatically delegitimize outcomes; it does demand literacy in how influence coagulates.

2. Ethical Clarity. When we can distinguish *secrecy as shelter* from *secrecy as leverage*, we can defend communities that must hide to survive—and expose those that hide to prey. The same analytical tools that map oligarchic patronage can also safeguard dissidents and stewards of endangered memory.

3. Cultural Memory. Symbols are not quaint relics; they are continuity devices. They stitch past to present, lubricate elite reproduction, and carry buried programs. Ignorance of the code is not innocence; it is simply malleability.

Part I: Ancient Roots of the Hidden Orders

Chapter 1: The First Keepers of Secret Knowledge

We're after the "first keepers"—the people who didn't just accumulate information but organized it, guarded it, and moved it forward under the cover of ritual, rank, and oath. That trail runs through three key theaters: the temple-schools of Egypt, the scribal houses of Mesopotamia, and the initiatory circuits of Greece. Then we'll dig into one compact case study: the Hermetic writings—the kind of slim corpus that launched centuries of rumor, commentary, and imitation.

Along the way, we'll treat secrecy not as a spooky aesthetic but as a technology: a set of rules for who gets what, when, and why. And we'll track how that tech became the seed stock for later lodges, brotherhoods, and "invisible colleges."

The Mystery Schools of Egypt, Mesopotamia, and Greece

Why "mystery schools" existed at all

Three pressures explain why ancient elites built close-held knowledge systems:

1. **Scarcity and status.** In worlds without mass literacy, writing itself was power. Whoever could read orders, tally grain, or interpret omens decided outcomes.

2. **Risk.** Astronomy, medicine, or statecraft done wrong could get a city starved, a harvest mistimed, or a dynasty cut off. Gatekeeping limited catastrophic amateurism.

3. **Ritual legitimacy.** Knowledge bound to gods felt safer than knowledge tied to mere opinion. Oaths and ceremonies "sacralized" the information and the people who held it.

> *Secrecy as a technology*: *control of access, pacing of disclosure, and prestige signaling. This is the underlying pattern that later orders imitate.*

Egypt: Temples as laboratories, archives, and theaters

What we can show.

By the Old and Middle Kingdoms, Egyptian temples weren't just worship sites—they were production hubs for calendars, medicine, and ritual knowledge. The **Per Ankh** ("House of Life") at major temples functioned as a scribal archive and teaching center; temple reliefs and ostraca point to a pipeline that trained novices in copying, reciting, and performing sacred texts. Priests rotated through service; initiates moved from menial ritual roles to more abstract domains like calendrics and liturgy. Astronomy supported agriculture and festival timing; pharmacological recipes were collated with incantations; and funerary knowledge (think **"books of going forth by day"**) trained the living to manage the dead.

How secrecy worked.

Three layers recur: public rites in the forecourts (music, incense, processions), inner practices for temple personnel (formulae, handling of cult statuary), and the most restricted operations in **naos** spaces (god statues, oracular sessions). Texts label dangerous knowledge as **nis.t** (hidden), and certain divine names were not for casual circulation. Initiatory language hints at "becoming the god"—a ritual identity switch best understood as a controlled cognitive frame: you act as Horus or Thoth to "do" the ritual correctly.

What did an initiate actually learn?

Reading and writing (hieratic; later demotic), temple choreography, purity codes, and the memory architecture to deliver long formulae precisely. They also learned **heka**—a term often mistranslated as "magic," better read as "operative speech/action," the ability to make ritual language effective.

Processional Plan of a New Kingdom Egyptian Temple

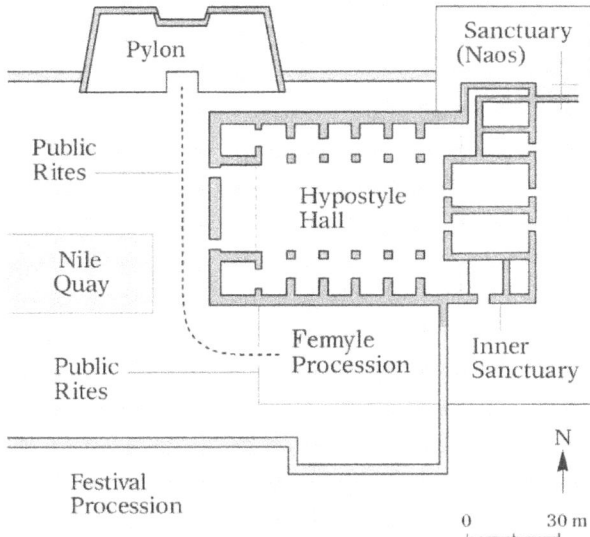

Pylon

Sanctuary (Naos)

Public Rites

Hypostyle Hall

Nile Quay

Femyle Procession

Inner Sanctuary

Public Rites

Festival Procession

N

0   30 m

The risk of overreach.

Don't project modern occult systems backward too far. There's no good evidence of lodge-style degrees or tarot-like symbol systems in pharaonic Egypt. What we do see is a strenuous mix of liturgy, performance, and elite schooling that later traditions will romanticize and reuse.

Mesopotamia: The edubba scribal houses and the omen machine

The edubba reality.

In Sumer, Akkad, and later Assyria and Babylonia, the **edubba** ("tablet house") trained scribes to copy sign lists, legal formulas, hymns, and epics. Clay tablets were filed in temple and palace archives; scribal families passed methods across generations. The specialization that matters for secrecy is divination: **barû** (extispicy), **āšipu** (incantation specialists), and later **ṭupšar Enūma Anu Enlil** (astral omen scribes).

The omen engine.

Long compendia like **Enūma Anu Enlil** link astronomical phenomena—eclipses, halos, planetary positions—to state outcomes: war, plague, succession stability. The method looks alien, but the social function is clear: it gave rulers a disciplined way to narrate uncertainty and justify policy. Crucially, "secret" tablets were flagged as such, and some were limited to palace or top temple circles.

Ziggurats and sightlines.

We don't need to over-mystify the ziggurat. It's a staged platform with a shrine on top—cosmic mountain imagery, yes, but also a practical observation point. What matters is the workflow: observation logs, omen lookups, ritual prescriptions—and the ethical codes binding who may speak with what authority in the throne room.

> *From raw phenomenon → encoded rule → court advisory. This three-step filter turns the sky into policy language, and the specialists become indispensable. Emphasize the role of written compendia as continuity devices.*

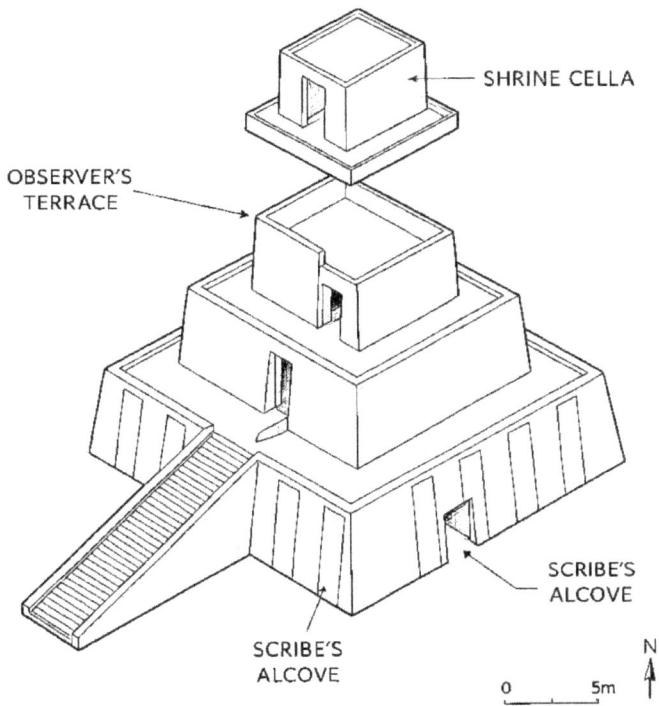

STEPPED ZIGGURAT—EXPLODED AXONOMETRIC

Power costs.

Monopoly on divination is fragile. When omens contradicted policy, diviners risked blame. To protect the guild, practitioners developed **procedural insulation**: strict formulas, rituals of purification, and the habit of quoting established lines—"the tablet says"—rather than staking personal opinion.

Greece: From open debate to closed doors

Greece gives us both the loudest public square and the most famous door-closing rites. Two tracks in particular matter:

Pythagorean/Orphic communities and the **Eleusinian Mysteries** linked to Demeter and Persephone. We'll treat Eleusis in depth in the next section, but first, the wider pattern.

Pythagoreans.

In southern Italy, Pythagorean circles combined mathematics, diet, and dress codes, and graded access to teaching. The structure is simple but potent: an outer layer hears lectures; an inner circle receives symbola (brief, often cryptic maxims) unpacked only orally. The goal wasn't just theorem knowledge; it was **character formation** to live in step with number and harmony. Secrecy guarded the pedagogy and the brand, plus safety, given periodic political backlash.

Orphics.

The Orphic strand, tied loosely to poems and gold lamellae (thin burial tablets), taught purification, ritual diet, and post-mortem travel instructions. The lamellae read like minimalist checklists for the soul's journey, with passwords and "do not drink from this spring" warnings—a travel protocol for the afterlife.

> *Evidence caution: Greek secrecy ≠ blank slate. We have inscriptions, commentaries, and some hostile reports (useful but biased). Treat claims of elaborate "mystery science" carefully unless they map to surviving artifacts or texts.*

Small Greek Andron (5th c. BCE)—

The Eleusinian Mysteries and the Cult of Isis

Eleusis: A city-sanctioned secret

What Eleusis was.

About fourteen miles from Athens, the sanctuary of Demeter and Kore (Persephone) ran an annual public-private hybrid: a festival all could see, capped by **mysteries** only initiates could experience. The polis managed it; the **Hierophant** and **Dadouchos** (torch-bearer) were hereditary roles; even Rome respected it for centuries.

The process.

Candidates (mystai) prepared in Athens, purified at the sea, and joined a long procession along the Sacred Way to Eleusis. Inside the **Telesterion**—a huge, roofed hall designed to hold thousands in stepped seating—initiates saw and heard what no outsider could. Ancient testimony insists there were **things shown (deiknymena), things said (legomena), things enacted (dromena)**. That triad tells you everything about the pedagogy: controlled multi-sensory learning designed to produce a memory that was both unforgettable and unspeakable.

What happened in there?

No spoilers exist—oaths held. But scattered hints suggest a climax built around light in darkness, a sacred object revealed (likely simple but symbolically loaded), and a recitation that re-keyed the myth of Demeter's loss and reunion. The point wasn't information but **transformation**: to align the initiate's memory and emotions with a religious timetable—loss, search, reunion—that promised a gentler post-mortem fate and a steadier present life.

*Anchoring claim: **Eleusis optimized memory.** The Mysteries weren't "mysterious" to be obscure; they were secret to be effective. Controlled sequence + sensory design = lifelong imprint.*

Why do governments tolerate this secrecy?

Because it worked. The Mysteries built civic unity across class lines; they were good politics. They also attracted visitors (and revenue). Secrecy didn't threaten the state; the state co-managed it. That's the blueprint for later "licensed" secrecy—ritual under civic umbrella.

What killed Eleusis?

A mix of religious change, imperial shifts, and physical destruction. But long before the end, the format had already gone diaspora—its logic copied by other rites.

The cult of Isis: Egypt rebrands for a Mediterranean market

From Nile to empire.

Isis began as an Egyptian goddess embedded in the Osiris cycle (wife, mother, mourner, magician). In the Hellenistic and Roman worlds, she became a traveling brand: **Iseums** (Isis temples) from Alexandria to Rome to the ports of Gaul, packed with hybrid iconography that Greeks and Romans could read—sistrum rattle, knot-tied robe, **Isis lactans** (nursing mother), and ship imagery for her role as protector of sailors.

Initiation in practice.

A rare literary window (a Roman-era novelist recounting his initiation in a temple of Isis) outlines purification, fasting, linen garments, ritual shaving, and a night ceremony culminating in "seeing the sun at midnight"—a stock phrase for ritual illumination in darkness. Again, secrecy is a feature, not a bug: the vow binds memory, and the memory binds identity.

Roman Iseum (Isis Sanctuary Courtyad, c.'stc CE

Why Isis caught on.

Three advantages: (1) **Portability**—the cult spoke Greek and Latin visually and ritually; (2) **Services**—it offered personal protection and clear ritual milestones; (3) **Inclusion**—women and non-elites could participate meaningfully. The package felt ancient and cosmopolitan at once.

Overlap without confusion.

Isis is not Eleusis, and neither maps perfectly onto later European fraternities. What carries forward are patterns: graded access, vows, sensory pedagogy, and the habit of assigning cosmic stakes to personal discipline.

Case Study: The Hermetic Texts and Their Coded Wisdom

What we're actually talking about

"Hermetic" in this chapter means the small Greek-language treatises and fragments from late antique Egypt and the Mediterranean world, attributed to **Hermes Trismegistus**—a syncretic mash-up of Greek Hermes and Egyptian Thoth. Think dialog pieces (teacher–student), short discourses, and a few technical notes. Add the Latin **Asclepius**, some excerpts preserved in other authors, and a separate, brief alchemical max-text later called the **Emerald Tablet**. The whole package is compact but generative—fertile soil for commentary.

The pedagogy inside the texts

Dialogues as gates.

The teacher delivers a vision (e.g., of the cosmos as Mind), the student balks, asks, and is led through conceptual "rooms." This is an **initiatory rhetoric**: you're not just told; you're brought to notice, then to assent, through staged questions.

Layering by vocabulary.

Key terms (**nous, logos, pneuma, gnōsis**) are familiar Greek words used with precise, elevated meanings. If you're "inside," you catch the force; if you're "outside," you read philosophy. That's code without

Hermetic ≠ Egyptian Old Kingdom. These texts are late, in Greek or Latin, written in a world already mixing philosophies. They reuse Egyptian themes but are not pharaonic manuals.

ciphers: a public text whose **operative** reading depends on trained distinctions.

Practices hiding in plain sight.

Between the metaphysics, there are behavioral programs: guard your speech, fast judiciously, attend to breath, contemplate the order of the heavens, and rehearse gratitude. These read like common-sense ethics, but inside the system, they function as **state-altering protocols**—ways to tune attention, calm reactivity, and make the teaching "stick."

Hermetic Lesson Engine

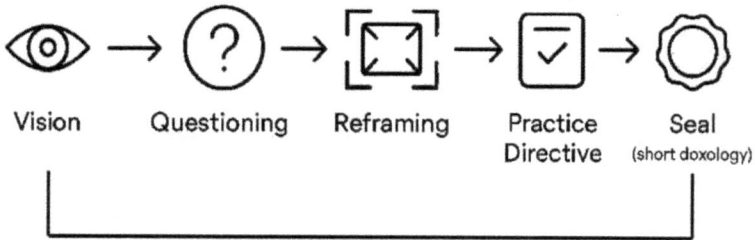

| Vision | Questioning | Reframing | Practice Directive | Seal (short doxology) |

"As above, so below"—clarifying the meme

The famous line in later handbooks compresses a simple claim: the **microcosm** (human) and the **macrocosm** (cosmos) mirror each other's order. The practical consequence is not fortune-telling but **method**: you can study the visible to infer disciplines for the invisible, and you can reorder the small (habits, attention, speech) to resonate with the large (reasoned order, proportion, cyclical time).

What's coded and what's not.

No acrostic puzzles or letter ciphers are needed to keep untrained readers out; the gating is cognitive. Without the vocabulary and the behavioral kit, you can't "do" the text, only summarize it.

Why Hermetica mattered to later secret orders

Portable framework.

Hermetic texts offer a compact cosmos, ethics, and a ritual tone that can be "installed" in new groups with minimal apparatus. You get (1) graded instruction, (2) a rhetoric of rebirth, and (3) a license to use symbols without demanding literalism.

Credential by antiquity.

Even when later readers misdated the material as unimaginably ancient, the **perception** of antiquity worked a stabilizing magic: "We belong to a chain of wisdom older than states." That's a powerful recruitment and retention tool.

*Operational point: **Hermeticism gives later fraternities a way to sound ancient while teaching modern disciplines of attention, speech, and self-rule.***

How Secrecy Actually Works (and Fails): A Field Guide

Before we close, I want a clear operational model. Treat this as the quick-glance kit you'll use throughout the book.

1) Admission.

Credentials (birth, sponsorship, skill) get you in the door. In Egypt: family line and temple schooling. In Mesopotamia: apprenticeship and proof of hand. In Greece: oaths and fees (and sometimes moral cleanups).

2) Pacing.

Not everything at once. You start with outer practices (copying, purifications, public rites), and if you hold the line—reliability over brilliance—you gain inner material.

3) Performance tests.

Most ancient secrets were **performative**: can you recite, time, mix, or observe? Written passwords mattered less than lived rhythms.

4) Social insurance.

Secrecy protects the group and the neophyte. If you fail, fewer people know. If the group is attacked, fewer targets are exposed.

5) Vulnerabilities.

Secrecy also hides rot. False teachers thrive when critique is outlawed; empty status rituals drift loose from skills; and myth can be weaponized.

Egypt in Practice: A Walkthrough from Novice to Insider

To make this concrete, let's "follow" a plausible novice through an Egyptian temple pathway.

Day 1–90: The Menial Stage.

You enter through a family connection. You clean floors, prepare incense, and fetch water from the sacred lake. A senior acolyte teaches you purity routines (washing, linen dress), the god's daily "feeding," and how to keep your mouth shut around visitors.

Months 4–12: The Script Stage.

You're copying short hymns and offering formulae in hieratic, learning the sign list by repetition. Your hand is judged for clarity. You memorize a simple astronomical cycle—when Sirius rises, when the Nile floods. You observe, don't speak.

Year 2–3: The Timing Stage.

You're entrusted with small cues: signal the conch at the right moment; carry the barque in procession without stumbling; light the lamp after a line, not before. If you "feel" the rite, they notice.

Year 4+: The Inner Stage.

If you have the temperament, you study in the Per Ankh. A priest shows you medical recipes paired with incantations and tells you why the pairing exists: to command the patient's attention, shape expectation, and reinforce the healer's authority. You copy a list of divine names and learn which names are for public litanies and which are to be held in reserve.

| Sweeping courtyarrd | Copying on on ostracan | Signaling in procession | Studying with a senior in an archive room |

Mesopotamia in Practice: From Clay to Counsel

The edubba grind.

You begin with sign lists, writing cuneiform wedges in neat grids. Your teacher raps your knuckles if you stray. You copy legal forms and debt records, practice math on base-60 problems, and eventually join a specialty track.

Choosing divination.

A master omen-scribe selects you if you show linguistic stamina and a calm temper. You copy omens word for word, learning not to improvise. You memorize stock phrases: "If the moon is haloed and Jupiter stands within, the king's enemies will…" Not prediction so much as **decision language**.

At court.

Under pressure, the high priest asks your team for counsel. You present options with ritual prescriptions ("perform a substitute king ritual," "propitiate Nergal"). Secrecy here protects the throne and the guild; leaks can cost lives.

Tablets are the memory, but the guild is the processor. *Destroy the people and the secrets die, even if the archive survives*

Greece in Practice: Initiation without illusion

Pythagorean rhythm.

You're silent for a year. You don't argue; you listen. You arrange your day by number—diet, sleep, exercise—so that your attention is trained. Only later do you see the geometry proofs. The point is ethical stability first, theorem second.

Orphic guidance.

You adopt a ritual diet and recite short hymns daily. You carry a small tablet with engraved lines for funerary use. It's not morbid; it's a program: remember who you are, where not to drink, and what to say if challenged. It's a **travel card** for a cosmology, not a ticket to a spectacle.

Eleusis restraint.

You swear and keep the oath. You don't gossip about the Telesterion. Outsiders always want to know. Insiders simply live as if the ritual "took." That is the point.

*Ethic to carry forward: **Take the oath seriously or skip the door.** In ancient systems, oath-breakers weren't edgy—they were unreliable.*

What Later Orders Borrowed—Precisely

I want to pin down the transferable mechanisms. Not slogans—operational features:

- **Graded disclosure.** Outer instruction, inner commentary, and a capstone experience. This appears in temple schooling, omen guilds, and mysteries alike.

- **Memory engineering.** Choreographed light/dark, rhythm, sound, and restricted speech to etch lessons into identity.

- **Credentialed speech.** The effective word (heka, logos) is not "just talk." The speaker's role, purity, and timing make it "operative."

- **Text + custodian.** Publicly accessible texts that only "light up" under a tutor. This scales learning without printing libraries.

- **Civic interface.** Functioning mysteries are rarely outlaw cults for long; they find a modus vivendi with the city or court.

Myths We Can Retire (and What to Keep)

Retire:

- A continuous, unbroken chain from pharaonic priests to modern lodges. The line is **broken and remade** many times.

- High technology codes in pyramids or ziggurats. The sophistication on display is organizational and ritual, not microchips or secret engines.

Keep:

- The deep pattern: elites build systems to conserve and transmit useful knowledge; secrecy protects training and status; ritual cements memory.

- The lived intensity: for initiates, these were not "themes"— they were life-ordering commitments.

Skepticism is a friend, not a spoiler. It filters nonsense while preserving real wonder at the scale and durability of human meaning-making

Scale & Timeline of Ancient Writing Media

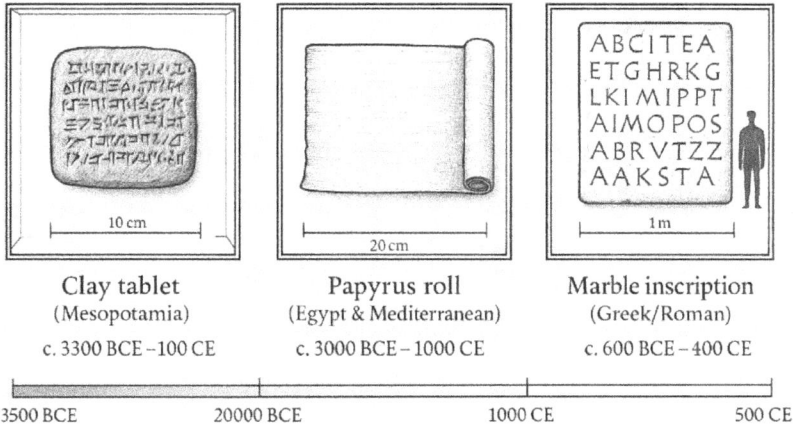

Clay tablet	Papyrus roll	Marble inscription
(Mesopotamia)	(Egypt & Mediterranean)	(Greek/Roman)
c. 3300 BCE – 100 CE	c. 3000 BCE – 1000 CE	c. 600 BCE – 400 CE

3500 BCE · 20000 BCE · 1000 CE · 500 CE

A Short Toolkit for Reading "Coded" Ancient Texts

When we later encounter charters, catechisms, and catechetical lectures in medieval or early-modern groups, use this toolkit derived from the ancient case studies:

1. **Identify the access gate.** Is there an oath, vocabulary test, or posture (silence) that "turns the key"?

2. **Map the sensory design.** Where are light/dark, sound/silence, or motion stillness used to mark transitions?

3. **Spot the public/private seam.** What can be said in the square vs in the room vs in the inner circle?

4. **Track the deliverables.** What competence or outcome justifies the secrecy? (Calendar, counsel, cure, character).

5. **Probe the civic contract.** Is the group licensed, tolerated, or hunted? That status shapes the ritual and the cover story.

Why This Matters for the Rest of the Book

We're not antiquarian tourists. We're building a baseline. Every later society in this book either **inherits** one of these early patterns or **reacts** against it. If you can recognize the Egyptian obsession with timing, the Mesopotamian conversion of sky to policy, and the Greek mastery of sensory initiation, you can read Renaissance, Enlightenment, and modern orders with clarity instead of guesswork.

Three closing signals to carry forward:

- **Secrecy is functional.** It's engineering for memory, identity, and group survival.

- **Myth rides on function.** Stories advertise and legitimize the function; they are not the function itself.

- **Continuity is curated.** Later orders pick the ancestors they need. That selection is itself a power move.

You now have the baseline: temples that trained minds like instruments, archive-schools that turned sky signs into royal decisions, civic rites that used secrecy to transform memory, and a set of slim texts that taught how to read the world as an ordered whole. This is the ground truth behind the later talk of "hidden masters" and "ancient brotherhoods." The real miracle isn't an immortal secret; it's the durability of a few simple methods: gate access, pace instruction, ritualize memory, bind speech to duty.

Carry these methods forward as we follow the thread into later centuries. When we meet an order that claims Egyptian pedigree, you'll ask: Where is their timing discipline? When a brotherhood says it guards the "astral sciences," you'll ask: where are their decision protocols? When a society boasts of a rebirth rite, you'll ask: how is the room designed to make a memory that sticks? That's how we'll keep our investigation honest and our curiosity sharp.

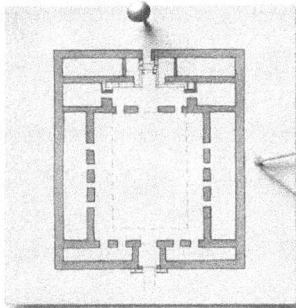

Egyptian temple plan (axial)

Cuneiform tablet (Mesopotamia)

Codex page (4th-6th c.)

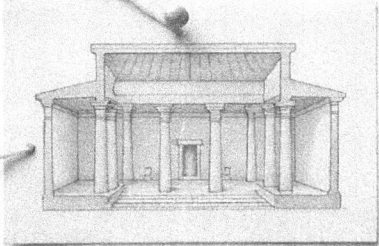

Telesterion cross-section (Eleusis)

Chapter 2

Priesthoods and Hidden Hierarchies

Open the case file for any civilization and you'll find two recurring fingerprints: a priesthood guarding access to power, and a sequence of gates—rituals, oaths, rooms-within-rooms—that sorts the initiated from everyone else. The story of "hidden orders" begins long before lodges and dossiers. It begins with specialists of the sacred who convinced communities that certain knowledge, certain spaces, and certain acts demanded a controlled chain of custody. That chain—subtle at first—hardened into hierarchies.

This chapter tracks how that mechanism worked on the ground. We'll walk through the worlds of Druids, Zoroastrian Magi, and working shamans. We'll unpack why initiations mattered, what made specific rites "forbidden," and how architecture—especially oracular chambers and underground sanctuaries—was engineered to bend minds and manage risk. Along the way, you'll see how to read these places like an investigator rather than a tourist: who controlled the door, who controlled the narrative, and who controlled the exit.

Priesthoods as Gatekeepers: Why Knowledge Went "Need-to-Know"

Priesthoods arise wherever three pressures converge: uncertainty (What will the seasons do? Why do people get sick?), scarcity (of grain, metals, healing), and spectacle (the ability to stage a result that feels more-than-human). If your group can forecast eclipses, time harvests, heal with plants others don't recognize, or put a trembling, truth-speaking oracle onstage, you don't throw that on an open wiki. You wrap it.

That wrapping takes forms we'll keep seeing:

- **Controlled access to the sacred**: groves, fire-altars, inner rooms, caves, or fenced-off precincts.

- **Controlled knowledge**: oral teachings with heavy penalties for leakage; the "right way" to speak, sing, measure, and mix.

- **Controlled selves**: initiations that break and remake identity so a person becomes a vessel that can carry the teachings under pressure.

When you control access, knowledge, and the self, you don't just run ceremonies; you run a hierarchy. And once a hierarchy exists, secrecy stops being "esoteric aesthetics" and becomes an operational necessity.

Druids, Zoroastrians, and Shamans Guarding Sacred Knowledge

The Druids: Oral Archives in Stone Landscapes

Classical writers called Druids the intellectual class among Celtic peoples: judges, diplomats, astronomers, healers, philosophers, ritualists. Whether they were a single pan-Celtic institution or a family of regional schools is still debated; what's clear is the method. They taught by voice, not parchment. Memory feats were the gate; decades of training were the filter. Oral transmission didn't just guard content—it trained the carrier. If you can recite cycles of law, poetry, cosmology, and star-lore in sequence, you're not a casual leaker.

Look at Britain and Ireland's megalithic precincts—stone circles, avenues, alignments—and you glimpse the classrooms and auditoria in which priestly specialists worked. The standing stones at Calanais (Callanish) in the Hebrides, for example, form a cross-shaped arrangement with an inner circle and long sightlines that track lunar extremes. Even stripped of later myth, the site reads like a tuned instrument for sky-measuring and calendrics, the kind of place where a trained specialist could "call" the heavens for a crowd and make it persuasive.

In this setting, the Druidic package—astronomy folded into law and healing; poetry as a memory technology; taboo (geasa) as social engineering—worked because the landscape cooperated. Groves were classrooms; circle centers were stages; causeways and mounds provided procession routes that dramatized doctrine. The secrecy wasn't theatrical. It was the IP strategy.

Druids: What to Remember
- *Oral transmission isn't a romantic flourish; it is a security model.*
- *Architecture cues belief: processional routes, sightlines, and acoustic pockets help ritual "land."*
- *The Druidic skill stack (law + sky + healing + performance) makes a priesthood politically indispensable.*
- *Sites like Calanais show the physical scaffolding that made the "invisible" hierarchy visible when needed.*

Zoroastrian Magi: Fire, Purity, and the Management of Cosmic Order

Move east to ancient Iran, and you find a different packaging of priestly authority around the fire altar. Zoroastrianism organizes the world into truth versus the lie (asha vs. druj), and the Magi, a hereditary priestly tribe, serve as technicians of order: tending ritual fires, reciting the Yasna liturgy, and policing purity rules that reach down into water use, corpse disposal, and even nail clippings. This is not mere fastidiousness. It is population-scale risk management framed as cosmic hygiene.

Behind the altar work is a data economy. The Magi curate calendars, auspicious timings, and astral knowledge that feed into kingship. That pipeline—the seat by the fire to the ear of the throne—makes priestly secrecy a state asset. Later, Iranian currents—Magi, Mithra worship, and philosophical blends—cross-pollinated with Gnostic and Manichaean movements that explicitly recruited intellectuals in Late Antiquity, giving Europe a model for "heretical" elite networks centuries later. At least one major modern synthesis traces these linkages through the Magi and Mani to later European currents of hidden doctrine, showing how a priestly caste's astral and moral technologies seeded shadow traditions downstream.

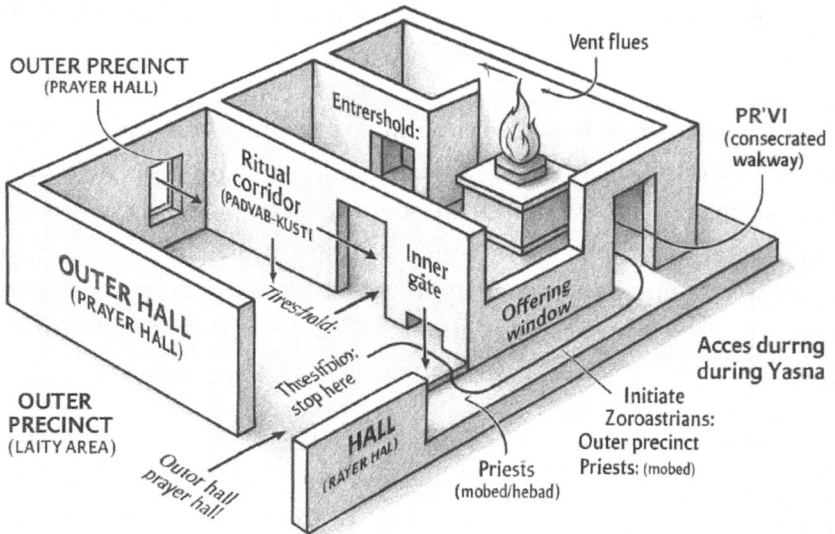

ZOROASTRIAN FIRE TEMPLE (ATASHCADEH) CUTAWAY: MOVEMENT DURING YASNA

Zoroastrian Gatekeeping
- *Purity rules are not "fussy"; they are social control dressed as hygiene.*
- *Calendar and astral knowledge feed royal decision-making.*
- *Heritable priesthood + liturgical monopoly = long half-life for hidden hierarchies.*
- *Iranian priestly models echo in later "secret" movements via intellectual lineages.*

Shamans: Field Operators of the Underworld

Unlike Druids (institutional) and Magi (hereditary), shamans are surgical. They serve bands, villages, or confederacies as brokers with other-than-human persons—animal masters, ancestors, local powers. Their legitimacy rests not on state sanction but on results: the fever breaks, the lost are found, the hunt succeeds.

Their architecture is portable: a drum, a costume, a controlled light-and-sound environment. But they also use fixed sites—caves, chasms, springs—where the "underworld" is acoustically and psychologically near. Many initiations are orchestrated ordeals of isolation, fasting, sensory overload, or deprivation. The secrecy here is partly safety (misuse of plants, risk of psychosis), partly intellectual property (songs, maps of the spirit-world), and partly liability: if a rite goes wrong, you want the public story contained.

Shamanic Secrets

- *Fieldwork, not doctrine, drives authority; secrets are operational, not philosophical.*
- *Caves and springs are not props: they are interfaces where acoustics, darkness, and humidity alter cognition.*
- *Initiation is a safety certification as much as a spiritual transformation.*

The Role of Initiation—and Why Some Rites Are "Forbidden"

Every serious priesthood uses initiations to do three jobs at once:

1. **Filter**: Only those who can endure hardship, keep silence, and follow cues get through.

2. **Imprint**: A sequence of sensory shocks, oaths, and stories is used to reframe the self's core narrative.

3. **License**: The new person is entrusted with procedures that can harm if mishandled (herbs, trance methods, rites that affect social cohesion).

The "forbidden" label is not only moral; it is **risk management**. Techniques that destabilize the psyche, manipulate crowds, or violate taboos require containment. That's why rites often live in controlled chambers—crypts, caves, vaults, and sealed rooms—where sound, smell, temperature, and oxygen can be tuned. That's also why some traditions insist on staging degrees in sepulchral or vaulted spaces with skulls, coffins, or "grave" symbolism: not to be macabre, but to induce a reversible death-of-the-old-self in a space that feels consequential enough to stick. Some high-grade European rites, for example, have historically conferred degrees in specially built vaults or cellar-like "sepulchral chambers," complete with bones, coffins, and funerary iconography designed to underscore rebirth into a new fellowship.

Case Study: Oracle Chambers and Underground Sanctuaries

We now look at four sites that show the hardware of hidden hierarchies: how an oracle is staged, how an escape corridor doubles as a power-preserving device, how an underground tribunal broadcasts terror, and how tiny "priest holes" win a cat-and-mouse game against a state.

Delphi: The Oracular Machine

High on Mount Parnassus, Delphi organized access to Apollo with ruthless efficiency. The public saw a pilgrimage: purification in the Kastalian spring, a procession along the Sacred Way lined with votive offerings, a sacrifice, and then a question submitted to the priests. Behind the scrim was a data operation. The Pythia—an older woman selected for probity—sat over a fissure and entered trance, while a priest framed the response in verse. The ambiguity of the replies was not laziness; it was a safety valve against political fallout. Kings sent lavish gifts; the oracle returned hedged counsel that, if read one way, could be called "accurate" after any outcome. Croesus learned this at the cost of his kingdom when he took "If you cross the river, a great empire will fall" to mean Persia's. It was Lydia's.

The rooms mattered. A fissure vented intoxicating gases; the tripod seat, the darkness, and the choreography of question-and-answer created an environment where outcomes felt fated. The site added layers—sporting festivals, treasuries, theaters—so the oracle's charisma could be embedded in a civic brand that made Delphi the Greek world's spiritual switchboard for centuries, even as control shifted under Rome and finally ended under Christian emperors.

The Passetto di Borgo: Survival Architecture of a Priest-King

Not all hidden passages serve metaphysics. Some preserve the office that houses it. In May 1527, as an unpaid imperial army—heavy with Lutheran mercenaries—sacked Rome, Pope Clement VII fled St. Peter's through a narrow, elevated corridor set within the old Leonine Wall, the **Passetto di Borgo**. Running roughly 800 meters to the fortress of Castel Sant'Angelo, the Passetto was camouflaged as battlements and even, at one point, as a mock aqueduct. Its windows, narrow and high, provided light and air without offering easy targets to the mobs below. That day, the Swiss Guard died buying minutes. Those minutes were enough. The papacy survived the sack because the corridor existed.

Seen through our lens, the Passetto is an "executive continuity" device that turns a sacred capital into a defensible campus. It's where ritual power meets crisis planning: a priesthood that rules must plan to run. The corridor's concealment within public architecture—read as wall, not as passage—shows how hidden hierarchies use the city itself as a cloak.

Passetto Lessons

- *Hidden orders invest in continuity; corridors are policies in stone.*
- *Camouflage is often "nothing to see here" architecture.*
- *The survival of a hierarchy sometimes depends on minutes, not miracles.*

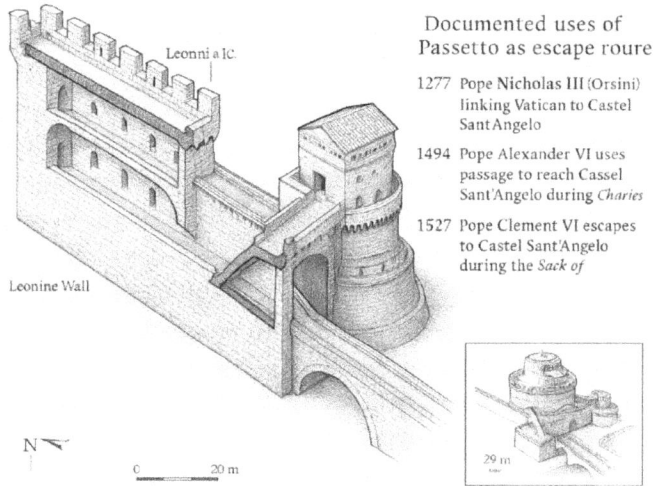

PASSETTO DI BORGO: AXONOMETRIC OF THE LEONINE WALL AND LINK TO CASTEL SANT'ANGELO (1277-1527)

Leonni a lC.

Leonine Wall

Documented uses of Passetto as escape route

1277 Pope Nicholas III (Orsini) linking Vatican to Castel Sant'Angelo

1494 Pope Alexander VI uses passage to reach Cassel Sant'Angelo during *Charies*

1527 Pope Clement VI escapes to Castel Sant'Angelo during the *Sack of*

N

0 _____ 20 m

29 m

The Grotto of the Beati Paoli: A Subterranean Tribunal of Fear

Beneath Palermo's Capo district lies a compromised riverbed turned catacomb complex. In local memory, this was the meeting place of the **Beati Paoli**, a hooded confraternity that operated at night, ambushing enemies in alleys and vanishing into the underworld. Their legend paints them as vigilàntes for the weak; historians suspect vendetta and power for its own sake. Either way, the grotto shows the physics of intimidation: steps down from an alley, curved walls, iron staples set into stone, and a chamber whose very isolation amplifies the feeling of being judged by an invisible law. No records were kept; an underground room and oral rumor were the media strategy.

Even if modern Mafia claims to descend from them are marketing, the grotto demonstrates the pattern: secrecy plus scenery equals authority. The tribunal's "courtroom" is the cave. The verdict is theater carried into the streets above by whispers.

Priest Holes: Micro-Architecture Against the State

When Elizabethan and Stuart authorities criminalized Catholic clergy in England, a tiny counter-architecture proliferated: **priest holes.** These were minuscule compartments—inside chimney breasts, under stair treads, behind paneling—designed to hide a person for hours or days while soldiers searched a house. Their designers mastered the art of misdirection: asymmetrical dimensions, false draughts to confuse smoke patterns, even decoy "bad" hiding places to burn search time.

This is a different hierarchy—a persecuted network rather than a public priesthood—but the principle is the same: space as a tool of secrecy. The hole itself is a sacrament of survival. The house becomes a liturgical object with hidden reliquaries; the rite is waiting silently while boots thump overhead.

An Alchemical Doorway: When a City Wall Becomes a Thesis

Not every sanctuary is subterranean. In Rome, a seventeenth-century noble's garden gateway, the **"Magic" or Alchemical Door,** was dressed with cryptic inscriptions and emblems from Rosicrucian lore—an advertisement and a shield for a laboratory quest to perfect matter and the self. The portal's iconography—glyphs, mottos, and a reproduction of a famous alchemical frontispiece—sends a message to the initiated: the "lab" is a temple, and the threshold itself is a test. It's a reminder that urban fabric can be hijacked by hidden hierarchies in broad daylight; discretion becomes a semi-public riddle.

The Ethics of Secrecy: What Was Being Protected?

It's convenient to imagine secrets as always sinister. Often, they were **protective:**

- **Protecting tools:** Plant combinations, anesthetics, and trance methods can be harmful in incompetent hands.

- **Protecting people**: Communities in danger needed "priest holes" and codes.

- **Protecting meaning**: Ritual impact degrades under overexposure. The strongest rites are one-time experiences; secrecy keeps them potent.

But secrecy also protects **interests**. When prophecy leans into politics, when purity rules become enforcement, when underground tribunals declare themselves the law, the same techniques that heal can dominate. That is why this subject demands a balanced eye: admire the engineering, audit the outcomes.

From Sacred Groves to Shadow Networks

By now, you can feel the continuity. The Druidic fusion of sky-law-healing, the Magi's custodianship of cosmic order, and the shaman's fieldwork all solved real problems with scarce skills. Initiation converted those skills into hierarchies; architecture made the hierarchies durable; narratives made them transmissible. The case sites we examined show the "back rooms"—how oracles were staged, how leaders were extracted, how fear traveled underground, how micro-spaces outfoxed a state.

In later eras, the same grammar writes itself into lodges, salons, chapels, and vaults. Some degrees still prefer cellars and sepulchral décor to make the inner turn feel irreversible; the point is not the theatrics but the **effect**: a structured change of identity calibrated by room, symbol, and script.

Strip away the costumes and you're left with a human constant: we build rooms to do hard things—heal, decide, crown, judge, survive—and then we build stories to protect those rooms. Priesthoods accumulate; hierarchies crystallize; corridors and vaults get cut. Sometimes the results are generous—law encoded in poetry, fire tended for the common good, a hole that keeps a life from ending on the scaffold. Sometimes they are stark: terror courts below, ambiguity repackaged as wisdom, purity rules turned into batons.

Understanding that the spectrum is the real initiation for this book. In the next chapters, the pattern will reappear with new actors and new technologies. Keep the lens: control of access, control of knowledge, control of selves. When you can map those, you can see the hidden order, whatever name it goes by.

Takeaways to Carry Forward

- *Hidden orders are not accidents; they are solutions to uncertainty, scarcity, and spectacle.*
- *Architecture is policy embodied: who enters, who waits, who sees, who knows.*
- *Initiation is a safety and identity protocol; "forbidden" often equals "dangerous if misused."*
- *Oracles and tribunals—sacred or shadow—work because logistics do.*
- *Continuity hardware (corridors, vaults, holes) keeps hierarchies alive through shocks.*

Chapter 3

The Occult Blueprint of Empire

If you want to understand how power endures, don't start with laws or swords—start with rites. Empires that last are empires that ritualize. They braid symbols, ceremonies, and sacred stories into the daily machinery of rule so thoroughly that obedience feels like alignment with the very order of the cosmos. In this chapter, we crack open that operating system.

We'll walk through three laboratories of imperial ritual—Babylonia, Persia, and Rome—and then go below street level in Rome to examine a single case study: subterranean Mithraic temples that ran like a parallel network beneath the formal civic cults. Along the way, we'll keep our eye on the same question: how does ritual power shape political power, and how do symbols make hierarchy feel natural?

Ritual isn't garnish on political power. It's the hidden scaffold that sets the rhythm, mood, and meaning of authority—turning commands into cosmic necessities and rulers into managers of fate.

Babylon: When the King's Tears Set the Calendar

Babylonia did not separate "state" from "cult." It didn't have to. The palace and temple were two desks in the same office, staffed by different specialists who shared the same mission: keep cosmic order steady and predictable so crops, floods, tax receipts, and military campaigns could be planned with confidence. The most important line in that mission: the New Year festival—Akītu.

The Akītu Logic: Humiliation, Reset, Renewal

Once a year, the king entered a ritual in which status was deliberately inverted. He was stripped of regalia, struck by the high priest, and required to present a confession before the statue of the city's patron god. The ideal outcome wasn't martyrdom; it was tears. If the king wept, it meant the god accepted him; order was renewed; the year could proceed. The theatrics mattered: the humiliation dramatized a truth rulers rarely admit—no one is above the cosmic rules. By acting that out, the king bought renewed authority to enforce rules on everyone else.

AKĪTU TAKEAWAY

Annual ritual vulnerability is not weakness in monarchy; it's a maintenance cycle. The public sees a sovereign who submits to law—then enforces it with moral credit freshly topped up.

Divination as Bureaucracy

Babylonian diviners weren't fringe mystics; they were civil servants. Omen series, liver models used in extispicy, and planetary observations fed into decision memos about war, irrigation, and taxation. The point wasn't superstition; it was standardized risk management. If the heavens were a spreadsheet, the diviners were the data analysts.

Sacred Property and Stone Warnings

Babylonian boundary stones (kudurru) were charters in basalt—grants of land recorded under the gaze of carved divine emblems. They end with curses against violators. In modern terms, it's a layered enforcement scheme: ritual sanctions (divine wrath), social costs (shame), and legal penalties (confiscation). The stone itself is a symbol that fuses all three.

ENFORCEMENT TRIANGLE

Babylonian enforcement stacked:
1. *Sacred deterrence (curses),*
2. *Social deterrence (honor/shame),*
3. *Administrative   deterrence   (fines/seizures).*
   Stacked sanctions cut enforcement costs.

Persia: Administration as Rite, Audience as Theatre

The Achaemenid Persian Empire's industrialized legitimacy. It stretched thousands of kilometers, yet made subject peoples feel seen. How? By staging the government itself as a ritual.

The Audience Scene: A Script for Loyalty

Persepolis' reliefs show delegations of subject peoples offering tribute. This was not casual decoration; it was the choreography of consent. The dignified procession standardized an experience: your people appear, your dress is recognized, your tribute accepted, and your place in the imperial mosaic affirmed.

Inscriptional Formulae as an Operating System

Achaemenid royal inscriptions hammer the same structure: the king acts "by the favor of the Wise Lord." The formula is compact: the king maintains order and truth (asha), the god legitimates success, and subjects prosper under that alignment. These aren't mere boasts; they are constitutional in spirit—statements of how authority is supposed to work and where it goes wrong (lies, disorder, rebellion).

Ritual Geography, Not Just Roads

The Royal Road gets praised for speed, but its deeper function was ritual synchronization. Posts equal predictability; predictability equals trust. Messages and tributes arrive on time, so festivals, tax cycles, and military assemblies hit their mark.

Fire and the Question of Cult

Public rhetoric emphasized the supremacy of truth, order, and divine favor, embodied in careful, repeatable acts at altars. Whether every modern term fits neatly is less important than the fact that visible, disciplined ritual framed the empire's image: clean, ordered, and just.

Apadana Audience: King, Winged Disk, and Sealed Tablet (Achaemenid Court Order)

Rome: Where Law, War, and Religion Share a Desk

If Babylonia fused temple and palace, Rome fused priesthood and politics. Roman officials took auspices, magistrates performed sacrifices, and the Senate consulted sacred books before major moves. The city's core question was never "Is this legal?" alone—it was "Is this legal and ritually correct?"

The Augur's Line and the Magistrate's Gaze

Augurs marked out a templum in the sky, watching for signs to greenlight or delay action. That wasn't mystical fog; it was a speed bump for impulsive policy. Ritualized waiting allows coalitions to stabilize, messages to spread, and tempers to cool while everyone says, with a straight face, "We're waiting on the birds."

The Suovetaurilia and the Military Calendar

Before campaigns, Rome performed the suovetaurilia—sacrifice of a pig, sheep, and bull—to purify land or army. The ceremony set the campaign's moral baseline. Armies swore the sacramentum, a binding oath tying soldier to commander and commander to the gods. You aren't just marching with a flag; you're enrolled in a contract with heaven.

Triumphs: Victory Converted into Civic Credit

The triumph wasn't a parade; it was a conversion ritual. Personal battlefield success is volatile capital—it can backfire as envy or fear. The triumph transfers a general's volatile glory into public stock. Spoils become temples, temples become holidays, and holidays become memories that renew the social contract.

ROUTE OF A ROMAN TRIUMPH

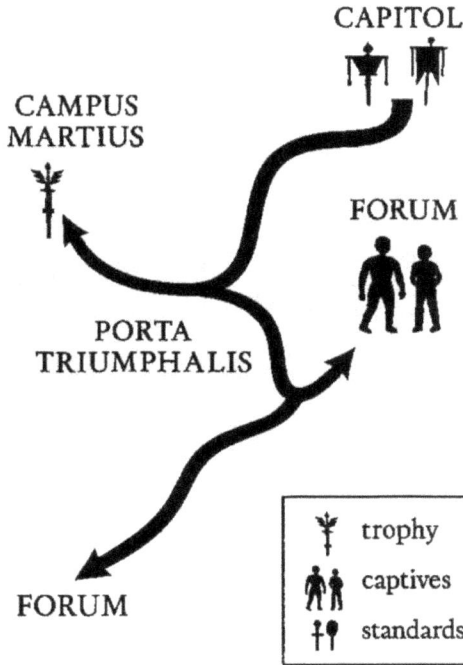

CAPITOL

CAMPUS MARTIUS

FORUM

PORTA TRIUMPHALIS

FORUM

trophy	
captives	
standards	

The Imperial Cult: Loyalty in a Civic Key

Honoring the emperor's genius in provincial temples knitted far lands into a common calendar. Attendance was a political belonging. By lighting a flame on the same dates across the empire, provincial elites aligned their reputations with the center's rhythm.

Symbols in the Senate and on the Street

Fasces (rods and axe) were carried before magistrates—portable reminders of lawful force. Standards (aquilae) concentrated legions' spirit into metal; losing one wasn't a tactical mishap—it was a spiritual wound. Purple dye, laurel wreaths, and curule chairs were not in fashion. They were coded messages everyone could read.

ROMAN SYMBOL LEXICON (ULTRA-BRIEF)

Fasces = lawful coercion
Eagle = legion's soul
Laurel = victory certified
Purple = authority tier
Lituus = ritual jurisdiction

EMBLEMS OF ROMAN POWER AND RITUAL

Fasces	Aquila	Laurel	Toga praetexta	Lituus
imperium's authority (*imperium*)	legion's eagle standard	victory wreth	purple-edged magistrate's toga	augural's staff

Embedding Symbols in Governance: How Ritual Runs the Machine

Collect the threads and you'll see the pattern. Ritual power works not because masses love incense but because managers love predictability, and rituals manufacture it.

Calendars: Time as a State Asset

Akītu reset Babylonian sovereignty; Persian audiences clustered around a court calendar; Roman fasti regulated market days, assemblies, and festivals. Control the calendar, and you control when people gather, trade, vote, and fight.

> ### GOVERNMENT'S TIME HACK
>
> *Calendars are silent laws. Whoever sets the feast days sets the work days—and the mood.*

Processions: Moving Law Through Space

From Babylon's processional way to Roman triumphs, leaders used processions to convert urban space into pages of a story. The city becomes a book you can read with your feet. Every turn, every gate, is a chapter.

Oaths: Glue for Large Systems

From the Roman sacramentum to Persian declarations before divine favor, oaths turn large, impersonal systems into teams. The words are less important than the public scene: witnesses remember, and reputation becomes collateral.

Architecture as Ceremony:

Ziggurats, Apadanas, and forums each staged authority. High places emphasize vantage and surveillance; hypostyle halls flatten crowds into orderly lines; basilicas slot disputes into lanes of speech. Architecture fixes behavior before words are spoken.

Coins and Seals: Pocket-Sized Sermons

Imperial messages shrink to hand-held media—coins and seals. An emperor's face, a victory type, a god's emblem—all travel as propaganda with every transaction. Pay your taxes, and you receive a sermon you can spend.

Case Study: The Mithraic Temples Beneath Rome

Now we go underground—literally. Beneath public basilicas, baths, and insulae, Rome hid a network of small, standardized temples: mithraea. They were not a state cult, not a street spectacle. They were intimate, disciplined enclaves where men gathered after work, ate in common, and moved through ranks of initiation.

What a Mithraeum Looks Like—And Why

Most mithraea were long, narrow rooms (spelea), shaped to feel like caves. Benches ran along both sides; a niche at the end displayed the tauroctony (Mithras slaying the bull), flanked by torchbearers. The cave form forced shoulder-to-shoulder proximity and focused attention forward. It turned every meeting into a lived diagram of hierarchy and unity.

The Icon Everyone Shared: The Tauroctony

No matter where you go in the empire, the core image repeats. Mithras grips the bull, a dog and snake reach toward the blood, a scorpion attacks the bull's genitals, the torchbearers flank the scene, and above, heaven's band of zodiac signs appears. Whether you read it as a cosmic map, an agricultural myth, a calendar, or all three, the message is order wrestled from chaos—shared, teachable, translatable.

Ranks and Roles: A Hierarchy You Can Climb

Mithraic grades typically included seven stations—often styled as Corax (Raven), Nymphus (Bridegroom), Miles (Soldier), Leo (Lion), Perses (Persian), Heliodromus (Sun-Runner), Pater (Father). The names vary by site, but the structure does a consistent job: it offers progression. In a city where social status was mostly inherited, mithraea created a parallel merit ladder. You could earn esteem, prove discipline, and belong to a table of peers.

Who Joined, and Why It Fit Empire

Soldiers, clerks, merchants, and imperial slaves are frequent in dedications. Why? Because the cult's logic mirrored their work. Long postings far from home, strict schedules, small teams, high trust—then an evening meal with ritual stories about loyalty and light. The mithraeum was a clubhouse for the empire's middle managers of order.

Secrecy vs. Privacy

"Secret cult" is the phrase everyone uses. More accurate: "private cult." Mithraea weren't grand; they were local and selective. Privacy kept meetings focused and reputation protected. Secrecy added prestige. But these were not nests of sedition. In fact, the discipline required to advance made members valuable to the system that paid their wages.

Rituals You Could Feel

Initiations likely included tests of endurance, blindfolds, ordeals of heat or cold—all bounded by trust. Meals were structured, readings timed, vows exchanged. Nothing "occult" in a modern sensational sense; everything controlled. The point was habit formation: program your body to sit still, stay alert, obey signals, and keep confidence. That's also the point of a strong unit in any bureaucracy or army.

Initiation—Five Quiet Stills

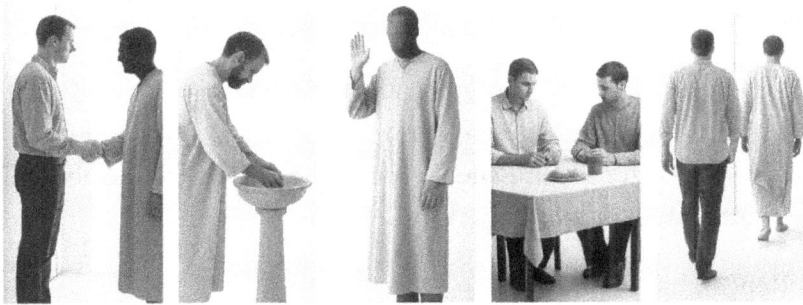

Threshold   Washing   Oath   Shared Meal   Dismissal
Greeting

A Network Below the Network

Because mithraea were copied and pasted across the empire, someone transferred know-how. Carpenters and stonecutters who built one could build another; rank badges, altars, and lamps traveled along trade routes. This standardized kit made mithraea predictable: walk in anywhere, and you know where to sit, how to behave, and what story you're inside.

Tension and Tolerance

As official civic cults shifted and Christianity gained ground in the fourth century, mithraea lost patrons and space. Some were repurposed; others sealed. Even so, the footprint they left—small, disciplined cells with shared rites—reveals a style of power that governments repeatedly rediscover: keep meetings small, roles clear, and rites repeatable.

The Toolkit: How Ritual Power Serves Rule

Let's close by naming the tools that empires used—and that other hidden orders love.

1) Calibrated Humiliation

Babylon's king submits once a year. Result: constant supremacy, the rest of the year feels legitimate. Leaders who ritualize vulnerability buy the right to act decisively afterward.

2) Repeatable Spectacle

Persian audiences, Roman triumphs: you know the script, you respect the script. Predictability makes magnanimity possible because it keeps envy and fear in check.

3) Sacredized Paperwork

From kudurru stones to sealed tablets and coins, documents carry iconography that persuades while they record. You read the law; you also feel watched by gods and ancestors.

4) Modular Spaces

Mithraea, basilicas, and courtrooms built to a template generate consistent behavior. Human nature isn't endlessly malleable; architecture directs it efficiently.

5) Oaths Over Force

Force is expensive; oaths are cheap. The more your system relies on sworn trust, the fewer guards you need. That's why armies swear, officials pledge, and guilds initiate.

Symbols and Ceremonies Embedded in Governance: A Field Guide

Because you're building a book that treats you as a co-investigator, here's a crisp field guide—what to look for in any empire or modern state claiming cosmic order.

Calendrical Mastery

Ask: Who sets intercalations, feast days, and public rest days? Are new regimes resetting calendars? That's a tell. If a ruler moves a major festival or creates a new one, you're watching a legitimacy play.

Processional Geography

Ask: Where do rituals move? Street plans that highlight palaces, temples, and arches are not neutral. Routes encode narratives. Follow the route and you've followed the message.

Regalia Grammar

Ask: What is carried in front of officials, worn on heads and shoulders, or stamped into metal? A society's symbol grammar can be learned like a language: fasces as syntax of lawful coercion; laurel as punctuation of victory; purple as capitalization of rank.

Ritual Pause Buttons

Ask: What are the formal reasons to delay the decision? Auguries, auspices, and omens serve the same managerial function as modern "cooling-off periods." If they vanish, expect volatility.

Parallel Networks

Ask: What private cults, guilds, or fraternities meet after hours? The healthier the bureaucracy, the more it tolerates disciplined private enclaves that stabilize morale. When regimes fear them, repression follows—and so does brittleness.

HOW TO READ POWER IN RITES
1. *Who sets the date?*
2. *Who writes the route?*
3. *Who owns the symbols?*
4. *Who can say "not yet"?*
5. *Who meets when the offices close?*

Investigator's Notebook
– Five Leads

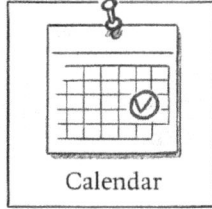

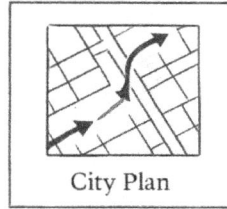

Calendar	City Plan
Regalia	Augur's Litius & Clock
Basement Door with Lamplight	Basement Door with Lamplight

Myths vs. Documented Influence: Keeping Our Balance

We need to be candid about evidence. Ancient states did not use "occult" in the modern sensational sense. They used rite, oath, and sign to stabilize the scale. When modern readers search for black-robed conspirators pulling strings, they miss the real story: the dull, repeatable, highly effective rituals that make complex societies governable.

That said, myths matter because elites believe them. If a king sincerely thinks his tears at New Year bind heaven to his reign, he will govern differently. If a Roman magistrate truly fears launching a policy without auspices, he will choose caution over glory. If a Mithraic initiate feels his rank ladder is the true measure of manhood, he will show up on time and keep secrets—at work and in the temple.

The Mithraic Subnet and the Imperial Mainframe—Why They Fit

This pairing is the heart of the chapter's claim. Look at what the state needs: punctuality, loyalty, team cohesion, and predictable emotion. Look at what mithraea delivered: punctual meetings, loyalty oaths, team meals, rehearsed endurance. No wonder soldiers, clerks, and merchants loved them. The cult didn't subvert the empire's needs; it trained men to meet them in a tighter key.

That's the blueprint's elegance: a public vertical (emperor → governors → magistrates) stitched together by private horizontals (lodges, collegia, cult cells). Top-down power needs side-to-side trust. The visible temples claim heaven for the city; the hidden speleae teach discipline to the citizens most needed to run it.

DISCIPLINE IS THE SECRET

Ritual doesn't conjure spirits; it conjures discipline. Discipline scales. Scaling is what builds empires

From Antiquity to Your Theme: Hidden Orders That Shape Destiny

The title of your book is a thesis: Shadow Networks Shape Outcomes. After studying Babylonia, Persia, Rome, and the mithraea, we can sharpen that thesis without overstating it.

1. Shadow networks don't replace formal power; they condition it.
2. Rituals inside those networks create the habits that institutions need.
3. Symbols allow those habits to feel meaningful, not mechanical.
4. Calendars make those habits repeat on schedule.
5. Architecture turns those habits into muscle memory.

Translate that into a modern or later context and you'll see the same gears: calendars set by institutions, icons worn by cadres, oaths sworn in private, processions that tell a city who's in charge, and under-the-radar rooms where the real bonding happens.

Practical Recon: How to "See" Rites in Stone, Script, and Space

For your investigative narrative, give the reader repeatable tools. Each empire teaches a technique the reader can apply in any city, museum, or ruin.

FIVE TESTS FOR A HIDDEN ORDER

— *Does it ritualize time?*
— *Does it mirror official hierarchies with its own ranks?*
— *Does it promise advancement by discipline?*
— *Does it use a standard space template?*
— *Does it glue members with meals and vows?*

- **Inscriptions:** Ignore flourishes; look for repeated formulas. Repetition is the law peeking through the poetry.

- **Processional Routes:** Find the straight lines and grand stairs. Ask what was carried along with them, when, and by whom.

- **Calendars and Fastis:** If you can't find them, look for market days, tax days, or festival markers. Power hides in schedules.

- **Rooms:** Measure with your eyes. Narrow? Bench-lined? Single focal niche? You're in a space designed for equalized seating and focused attention—classic for private rites.

- **Icon Sets:** One central image plus fixed side figures (like the tauroctony with its helpers) means you're looking at a teachable story kit.

The Quiet Symphony That Holds an Empire

Take a final, clear view. Babylonia's king is weeping on cue. Persia's courtiers file in perfect order. Rome's augur lifts his staff and says, "Not yet." In a basement under a Roman street, a group of men in a low, lamp-lit room recite an oath, share a meal, and promise each other steadiness. It's not mysticism in the modern sense. It's ritualized management of risk, emotion, and time.

Empires write their constitutions in stone and story. The stone directs bodies, the story directs minds, and the ceremony directs both. Under those layers, small private rooms train the people who make the system run. That's the occult blueprint of empire—not magic tricks, but the slow magic of repetition.

FINAL TAKEAWAY

Power lasts when it does three things at once:
— binds itself to a story bigger than itself,
— repeats that story in public on a schedule,
— and teaches that story in private to people who matter.

Part II: Medieval Orders and the Rise of Shadow Networks

Chapter 4: The Knights Templar

You've opened one of the most controversial files in the archive. The Knights Templar weren't just crusader horsemen in white cloaks; they were a military-religious corporation with a Europe-wide footprint, a finance arm that could move money more safely than kings, and a brand powerful enough to spawn centuries of rumor. In this chapter, we keep two tracks running at once: the paper trail (charters, trials, transfers of property) and the smoke trail (treasures, secret rites, curses). Wherever legend diverges from the record, I'll flag it clearly and show you why.

Origins in Jerusalem and the Crusades

The Templars begin as a problem-solving unit in a dangerous place. In the 1110s, pilgrim traffic to Jerusalem was booming, but so were ambushes on the roads to the holy sites. A small band of knights led by Hugues de Payens sought the king's permission to operate as a sworn militia to protect travelers and key routes. They were quartered on the Temple Mount, in buildings adjoining the former al-Aqsa complex—hence their name, "Poor Fellow-Soldiers of Christ and of the Temple of Solomon."

Cistercian allies helped transform the experiment into an institution. A council in the 1120s standardized their rule, emphasizing paradox: monks who fought, warriors who fasted. They accepted vows of poverty, chastity, and obedience, but unlike cloistered orders, they lived in garrisons, rode out in columns, and died in formations. From that scaffolding, they built a continental network: commanderies (local houses) to recruit, supply, and fund, and a set of fortified nodes across the Levant to project force.

What made them formidable was doctrine and logistics. Doctrine: disciplined shock cavalry—tight formations that hit hard, then yielded space for allied contingents. Logistics: a trans-Mediterranean supply chain that could feed ports, castles, and field armies. The order's master in the East was a theater commander; the master in the West ran recruitment and finance. That split-brain—operations there, resourcing here—was new.

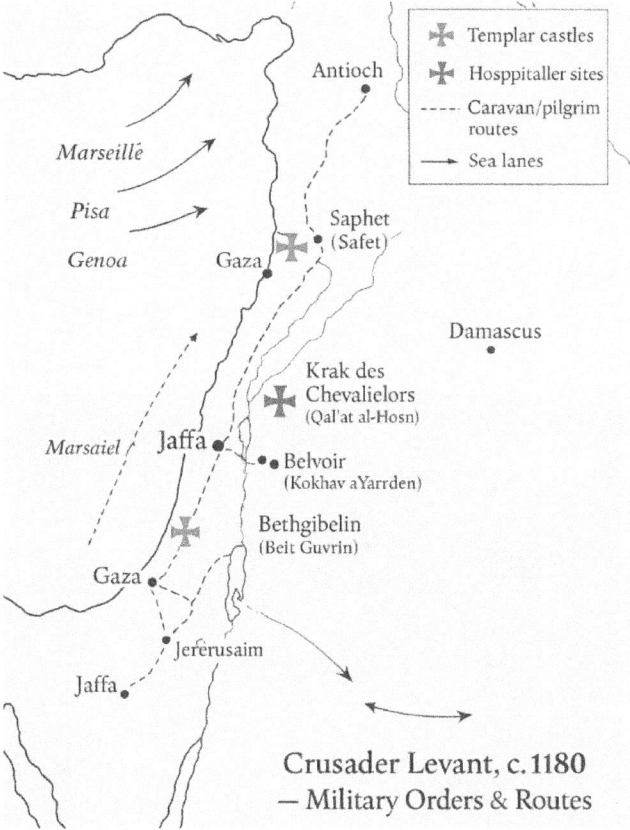

Crusader Levant, c.1180
— Military Orders & Routes

The Money Engine Behind the Cross

Crusading demanded liquidity. The Templars built a mechanism to move value fast and quietly. Donors gifted land and rents across Europe; commanderies converted that into grain, wool, and coin; the

Paris Temple functioned like a central treasury. Pilgrims could deposit funds in London and redeem them in Acre through coded instructions—a medieval "letter of credit." Kings used them, not because they loved monks, but because the Templars had the staff, vaults, and reputational capital to do what fragile royal exchequers could not: hold, audit, and disburse on time.

That reputation also made them targets. The larger the balance sheets, the louder the whispers: *Where is all that silver going?* In the absence of annual reports, mythology rushed in.

How a Templar "Letter of Credit" Worked

- *Pilgrim deposits coin at a local commandery; clerk records amount with a cipher and symbol.*
- *Messenger carries a nota (no precise sum written) to the Levant; receiving house verifies through codebook and counter-marks.*
- *Payment made in local currency minus a handling fee; ledger in Europe updates at quarter-year.*
- *Risk managed by diversification (many small deposits, many houses), not by modern insurance.*

Single-Page Flow Diagram

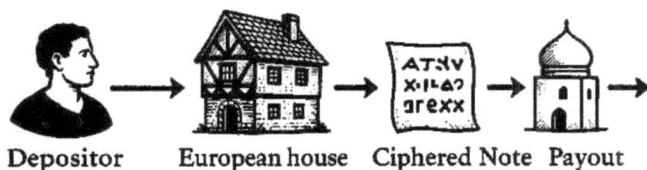

Depositor → European house → Ciphered Note → Payout

Alleged Hidden Treasures and Forbidden Rituals

Rumor is oxygen around closed doors. Three clusters of claims follow the Templars everywhere:

1. **A hidden hoard** was spirited away at the collapse.

2. **Heresies and blasphemies** at initiation;

3. **Esoteric transmissions** linking them to later brotherhoods.

Let's separate what the paperwork actually shows from what later storytellers embroidered.

What the trial records suggest about "forbidden rites"

A major strand in the charges against the order alleged that some novices were required to deny Christ symbolically and abuse a crucifix during reception—shocking claims for a Christian knighthood. The surviving interrogation material, inconsistent and often taken under duress, nonetheless points to pockets where something like this *did* occur. The best synthesis from an archival study argues it was not uniform, likely limited to a minority of houses, but real in those places, possibly as a hard-edge bonding act or to test obedience in secrecy.

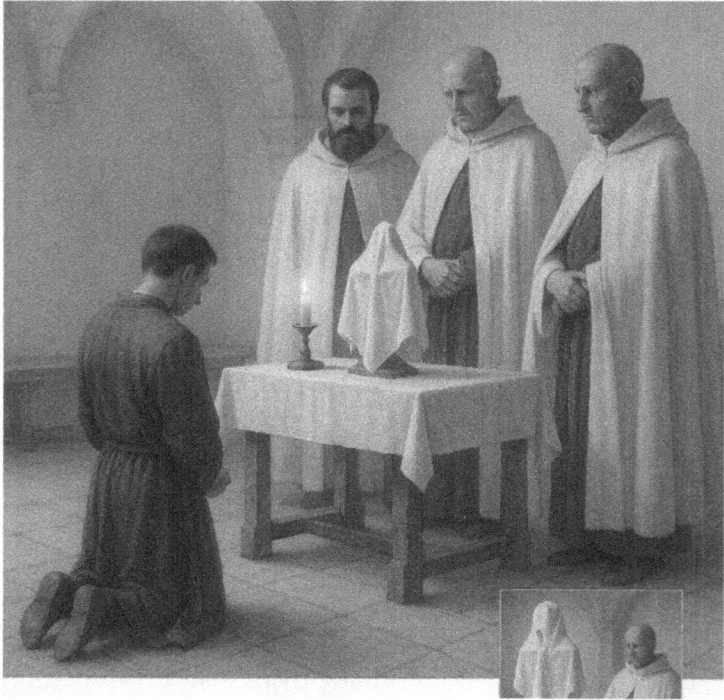

Early 14th-Century Chapter-House Profession (Western Europe)

Myth vs. Ledger (Rosslyn & Rennes)

- *Rosslyn built 1456; Templar suppression 1307–1312. Timeline mismatch is fatal to "Templar vault" claims.*
- *Rennes legend: provably modern embellishments and planted "evidence" created a lucrative fiction.*

Treasure and the Grail—myths that sell tickets

Two tourist magnets in particular are forever yoked to the Templar hoard: **Rosslyn Chapel** in Scotland and **Rennes-le-Château** in France. The timeline itself kills Rosslyn: it was founded in the 1450s—**a century and a half after** the Templars were suppressed—by a family who actually testified against the order in 1309. The carvings are gorgeous; their "green men," alleged New World corn, and "Masonic codes" have sober architectural explanations and later restorations that account for the peculiar details. No vault of Templar gold, no Grail.

Rennes-le-Château's mystery collapses into a 20th-century confidence game: a cash-strapped priest's mass-selling scam, forged parchments, and a modern self-styled "Priory" leader weaving in Merovingian bloodlines. It's a masterclass in myth-manufacture, not medieval banking.

The "Templar line" into later societies

A number of Masonic systems—especially in 18th-century Germany and Scandinavia—claimed secret succession from the medieval order. One elaborate stream, the **Swedish Rite**, dresses high-degree members in Templar-style habits, awards a ring of profession, and narrates a hidden priesthood lineage from a relative of Jacques de Molay. These claims are part of a beautiful and meticulously staged esoteric system, but they are not a direct medieval continuation; they originate in Enlightenment-era myth-making (Baron von Hund's Strict

> *"Do the Templars still exist?"*
> - *The medieval order was suppressed; there is no evidence of uninterrupted survival as a corporate body.*
> - *Later groups borrow symbols, rites, and names— sometimes with state honors—but are new creations with Templar-themed identity.*

Observance, etc.). The interesting twist is that in Sweden, the *state itself* recognizes a small chivalric order with Templar flavor—giving ceremonial legitimacy to a mythic inheritance. That's about modern crown patronage, not medieval survival.

The Sudden Destruction

Friday, 13 October 1307. Pre-dawn in France, royal sergeants arrive at Templar houses with sealed orders. The charges are sweeping: heresy, indecency, idolatry, and financial crimes. Shock arrests net hundreds. Why then? Why like this?

- **Politics and debt.** France's crown needed cash and control. The order held property, records, and independence that the king couldn't easily penetrate.

- **Jurisdiction games.** By moving first, the crown forced the papacy to chase, not lead.

- **Narrative warfare.** The salacious nature of the accusations— spitting on the cross, illicit kisses, worshiping a head— poisoned the Templars' moral standing before any court convened.

Trials varied by realm. In many kingdoms outside France, the proceedings were slower, less brutal, and often skeptical. Ultimately, the papacy suppressed the order (1312), transferring most property to the Hospitallers—on paper. In practice, local magnates and kings helped themselves. In Portugal, former Templar assets and personnel coalesced into the **Order of Christ**, chartered under new terms—more a legal workaround than a straight continuation.

Case Study: The Burning of Jacques de Molay—and the Curse That Followed

The scene. Paris, March 1314. After seven years of arrests, hearings, and staged reconciliations, the last Grand Master, Jacques de Molay, is brought to a platform on the Île de la Cité with other senior officers. A sentence of perpetual imprisonment is expected. Instead, de Molay speaks—rejecting confessions extracted under pressure and asserting the order's innocence. That outburst forces the hand of the authorities. By evening, a pyre is prepared.

Eyewitness accounts agree on the essentials: execution by fire, the Master facing Notre-Dame, dying unwavering. The **"curse"**—the dramatic claim that from the flames de Molay summoned Pope and King to appear before God within a year—is a story layered in after the fact by later chroniclers. It fits too neatly: Pope Clement V dies within weeks; King Philip IV within months. The coincidence amplified the legend, but the rhetorical speech as popularly quoted doesn't appear in the earliest, most reliable dossiers. The best reading is that a **powerful moral narrative** formed around real deaths and real timing, then hardened into "the curse of the Templars."

What Survived—and What Didn't

> *Legend vs. Record: De Molay's Last Words*
> - *Record: Execution by fire in Paris (March 1314); de Molay repudiates coerced confessions at the scaffold.*
> - *Legend: Fiery malediction summoning Pope and King; later sources amplify it.*
> - *Aftermath: Clement V dies in April 1314; Philip IV in November 1314—chronological fuel for myth-making.*

The order's **structure** did not survive. The **skill set** did. The Templars set templates that others followed:

- **Military-religious governance.** Later orders professionalized the model, from Malta to the Baltic.

- **Distributed finance.** Routine use of letters of credit, multi-house accounting, and trusted couriers seeded practices that merchant banks adapted.

- **Mythic capital.** No medieval order's brand value has compounded longer. That brand, however, is not the same as institutional continuity.

When modern groups claim descent, evaluate two things:

1. **Paper continuity**—charters, property, unbroken governance (there is none from the medieval Temple).

2. **Ritual continuity**—symbols, stories, degrees (abundant, but crafted centuries later). The **Swedish Rite** case is especially instructive: elaborate Templar-themed rites culminating in a monarch-bestowed knighthood give modern, ceremonial **legitimacy**, not medieval corporate survival.

Inside the Commandery: Daily Life Without Romance

Strip away the romance and you see a professional community:

- **Morning offices** and Mass;

- **Stables and armory checks**—the horse was your survival.

- **Training**—lance drills, formation practice, bow or crossbow, depending on theater;

- **Administrative chores**—rents collected, ledgers balanced, correspondence in a clerk's hand;

- **Supply logistics**—barley for horses, salt pork for men, and an obsession with fodder and shoeing.

This is not a mystical monastery so much as an **ops center** with prayer. Yes, relics and chapels mattered; yes, there were internal feasts and a culture of honor. But the engine room was practical: feed the brothers, pay the farriers, mount up.

How the Shadow Network Emerged

The Templars demonstrate a recurring pattern in hidden orders:

1. **Central mission justifies exceptional privileges.** (Protect pilgrims → tax exemptions, legal immunities.)

2. **Privileges create opacity.** (Independent courts, sealed accounts.)

3. **Opacity breeds suspicion.** (Rumors amplify; enemies compile dossiers.)

4. **A shock event triggers liquidation.** (Coordinated arrests; narrative of moral rot.)

5. **Myth rushes into the vacuum.** (Curses, treasures, secret heirs.)

Once you recognize the pattern, you can see how later groups—some secular, some spiritual—adopted the same operating logic. The legacy of the Templars is therefore double-edged:

- **Technical legacy:** logistics, finance, disciplined force.

- **Narrative legacy:** a bottomless reservoir for "hidden order" storytelling.

Frequently-Misread Evidence (and Why It Misleads)

- **Carvings read as codes.** Beautiful Gothic ornament is not a cipher unless you can show a chain of meaning that maps across multiple sites, dates, and craftsmen. Rosslyn's "green men," corn, and "Master/Journeyman/Apprentice" pillar names have conventional explanations and, in the case of the pillar names, late invention.

- **Documents planted or forged.** Rennes-style "discoveries" often crumble under paleography: ink, hand, spelling norms, and parchment age.

- **State-recognized "Templars."** Scandinavian chivalric forms with Templar styling are modern constructs, fascinating in their own right, but not medieval inheritances.

What the Templars Teach Us About Power

First, scale attracts scrutiny. Whatever your mission, the larger your footprint, the more someone will make it their mission to cut you down.

Second, secrecy must be traded for accountability at intervals. Total opacity is a short-term advantage and a long-term liability.

Third, narratives outlive institutions. If you don't curate your story while you exist, someone else will write it after you're gone.

Field Notes: Sites, Objects, and Archives (for your research team)

- **Paris Temple (site lost, records remain):** crucial for understanding the finance hub model.

- **Commandery remains across Europe:** stones tell you less than archives, but layout patterns repeat.

- **Trial registers (where available):** compare testimony clusters by region; chart which allegations repeat and where they don't.

Closing the File

The Knights Templar were not the keepers of every mystery attributed to them. They were more interesting than that: a prototype of disciplined, transnational power—military, financial, and administrative—operating inside a religious frame that gave them mandate and cover. They rose by being useful; they fell by being indispensable to the wrong debtor; they live on because the void they left begged for stories.

The smart way to write about them is the way you've seen here: keep the ledger and the legend side by side, and don't let either bully the other. The history is bracing enough to stand on its own—and the myth, properly bounded, adds texture to why the Templar name still sells out tours, novels, and headlines seven centuries after the last Grand Master faced the fire.

Chapter 5

The Rosicrucian's and the Quest for Hidden Wisdom

If you were standing in a small German print shop in the 1610s, you'd have felt it: the hum of rumor, the scent of oil and ink, and a stack of pages that seemed to promise a revolution without an army. Those pages—anonymous, learned, defiant—announced a brotherhood that claimed to heal the sick for free, renew all arts and sciences, and reform a war-weary Christendom. No names. No addresses. Only signs, emblems, and a story about a mysterious founder who had traveled to the East, mastered hidden knowledge, and then vanished into a seven-sided vault that would open "after 120 years."

That is the Rosicrucian puzzle. It is not a single society in the familiar sense, but a script for one—a design pattern for a network that could remain invisible, inspire action, and be endlessly re-created. To read the Rosicrucian texts carefully is to watch a new kind of "shadow network" come alive on paper: literate, moralistic, technically curious, theologically provocative, and perfectly suited to an age of censorship, plague, and war.

Rosicrucianism begins as a publishing event, not as a membership roll. The "order" is first and foremost a set of manifestos (1614–1616) that invite readers to become the network.

The Common Press & the Rose-Cross Dispatch (c. 1650)

The Secret Manifestos of the 1600s

Between 1614 and 1616, three texts appeared in the German lands that triggered what contemporaries called a "furore":

- **Fama Fraternitatis** ("The Fame of the Brotherhood"), 1614.

- **Confessio Fraternitatis** ("The Confession of the Brotherhood"), 1615.

- **Chymische Hochzeit Christiani Rosenkreutz, Anno 1459** ("The Chymical Wedding of Christian Rosenkreutz, 1459"), 1616.

The first two read like a cross between a press release and a spiritual indictment. They tell the life of **Christian Rosenkreutz (C.R.C.)**, a near-mythic German adept who travels through the Levant and North Africa in search of wisdom; returns with a reformed, Christianized hermetic philosophy; and founds a small fraternity devoted to charity, science, and piety. They outline simple rules (secrecy, free healing, modesty), and promise a coming renovation of learning. The third book, *The Chymical Wedding*, is a surreal, satirical, and deeply allegorical narrative of initiation—part romance, part laboratory dream—packed with puzzles, measurements, musical cues, and architectural details. It is the book that teaches you *how to read* the other two.

What made these texts explosive was not occult fireworks but their **tone**: practical, reformist, Christian, and sharply critical of empty scholasticism. They do not hawk talismans; they call for **better medicine** and **experimental knowledge** in the service of God and neighbor. They also promise a fraternity that will never pass a collection plate.

RULES OF THE FRATERNITY (AS REPORTED IN THE MANIFESTOS)

1. *Live and work without distinctive costume; remain unrecognized.*
2. *Heal the sick gratis.*
3. *Meet annually in the "House of the Holy Spirit."*
4. *Seek no worldly rank or wealth; practice a learned modesty.*
5. *Preserve the society through secrecy and the written record.*

Five Rules:
Simplicity, Care, Hospitality, Non-Domination, Study

    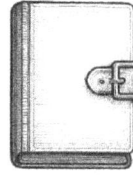

Simplicity   Care   Hospitality   Non-domina-   Study
                                          tion

The Response Literature: How Europe Read the Rose-Cross

The pamphlets did what well-timed manifestos always do: they split readers into camps and sparked a conversation that ran along postal routes and university corridors.

- **Supporters** argued that the fraternity was real, benevolent, and aligned with a Christian humanism ready for laboratories and lenses. They wrote in to volunteer, to defend the fraternity's orthodoxy, or to propose how the promised reform might work in practice.

- **Skeptics and critics**—including established alchemists and theologians—denounced the manifestos as a dangerous satire, a recruiting ploy, or a diabolical trick dressed in pious language.

Either way, the reaction networked scholars across Germany, the Low Countries, England, and France, all without a central office. That is the Rosicrucian trick: **circulate a myth of organization** and let the Republic of Letters build the organization itself—through reading circles, friendly societies, experiment clubs, and coded correspondence.

Alchemy, Mysticism, and Coded Philosophies

To understand the Rosicrucian program, you need the operating system underneath it: a late-Renaissance **Christian hermetism** married to **Paracelsian** medicine and to the conviction that creation is a set of **correspondences** waiting to be read rightly. The crucial moves:

1. **Nature is a text.** Metals, plants, and stars are letters in a divine script; laboratory work is exegesis with fire, glass, and balance.

2. **Microcosm and macrocosm.** The human is a miniature cosmos; what is healed in the body mirrors what can be reformed in the state and the churches.

3. **Experiment as piety.** The good physician is both technician and moralist—he cures bodies and mends the commonwealth. Knowledge without neighbor-love is counterfeit gold.

4. **Ciphers and emblems.** Truth is veiled partly for safety, partly because veiling is a teaching method. If you can follow the emblem, solve the acrostic, and reconstruct the geometry, you are ready to be trusted with more.

5. **A timeline of hope.** History is providential and expects a renovation—a "reformatio" that includes universities, courts, and workshops. The Rosicrucian manifestos place their bets on a near-future turning.

The Vault as a Diagram of Knowledge

The **Fama's** most cinematic moment is the discovery of C.R.C.'s subterranean vault "after 120 years": a heptagonal chamber with each wall engraved, a perpetual lamp (symbolic), a central altar bearing inscriptions, and documents carefully preserved. Read literally, it is a tomb. Read functionally, it is a **blueprint:**

- The seven walls = the seven planets/metals/virtues—a **curriculum**.

- The lamp = **unceasing study** and divine illumination.

- The sealed writings = **version control** for a research program—notes, experiments, and admonitions that survive regimes.

- The inscription ("After 120 years I will open") = **an internal**

clock built into the myth; the vault opens when **readers are ready**.

Coded Philanthropy: "Heal the Sick Gratis"

It is easy to miss how **practical** the manifestos are. "Heal the sick for free" is not a slogan for miracle shows; it is a policy plank. The movement calls for **cheap, effective remedies** and **new methods**: distillates, minerals, and botanicals used with careful observation, record-keeping, and peer scrutiny. This is early modern **outcomes research** in a religious key. The code and the allegory protect the discussion from censors; the charity requirement protects it from quacks.

Case Study: *Fama Fraternitatis* and Its Mysterious Authorship

What the *Fama* Says

The *Fama* reads like a short dossier:

- **A biography** of Christian Rosenkreutz: orphaned nobility; travels eastward (Damcar, Fez, Spain) gathering mathematical, medical, and hermetic teachings; returns to form a **small, disciplined circle.**

- **A rulebook:** secrecy, itinerant service, the annual home-meeting, and a rejection of vanity.

- **A discovery:** 120 years after the founder's death, the brothers open his vault, recover his intact body and writings, and decide to go public—**carefully**—through the *Fama* itself.

- **An invitation:** not to send money or visit an address, but to adopt a way of life and to **write back** in learned print to prove understanding.

Who Wrote It?

The authorship question is deliberately tangled—by design. The best way to understand it is to separate the **literary device** from the **likely workshop** behind it.

- **The device**: anonymity creates a universal "we." Readers in Wittenberg, Leiden, or London can imagine the fraternity exists near them, among them, or **as them**.

- **The workshop**: the style, theology, and humor of *The Chymical Wedding* point strongly to a brilliant Lutheran writer who later referred to that text as a **"ludibrium"**—a "playful mockery" with serious purpose. That is not a confession of fraud; it is a writer admitting he used **fiction as a surgical instrument** to cut away empty learning and tempt the teachable toward a reformed philosophy.

The likely scenario is a **circle** of learned friends in the southwest German intellectual sphere—students, pastors, lawyers—who shared Paracelsian interests, humanist reading, confessional anxieties, and a reformist itch. In that environment, attaching a real, fixed author to the *Fama* would have ruined the point. A single author can be silenced. A **program** can't.

Reading the *Fama* as a Design Document

Take the *Fama* not as a chronicle but as a **spec**:

- **Membership**: defined by practice (charity, secrecy, research) rather than by initiation rites available at a particular address.

- **Governance**: the annual "House of the Holy Spirit" functions like a **conference**—reports, peer review, and assignment of itineraries.

- **Infrastructure**: the vault is an **archive**, the code-phrases are **identity protocols**, and the call for letters is an **API** to the Republic of Letters.

That reading explains *Fama*'s strange power. It turns the **printing press** into an initiation hall and the **European postal system** into a lodge.

What Was New—and What Was Not

New

- A brotherhood defined primarily through **public texts**.

- A reform agenda that wove **laboratory method** into Christian moral life.

- A deliberately **scalable** network design: small cells, shared rules, shared myths.

Inherited

- The Hermetic conviction that the world is legible.

- Medieval charitable ideals reframed for a post-plague, pre-industrial Europe.

- Esoteric pedagogy: **veil as curriculum**.

How the Rosicrucian Myth Engineered a Shadow Network

1) Publishing as Initiation

The manifestos invert the usual secret-society logic. Instead of recruiting through private oaths, they **publish** and wait for the right readers to **self-select**. The act of correctly decoding, replying in learned prose, and setting up a local circle essentially performs the initiation. This is stealthy, **cheap**, and highly **resilient**.

2) Ethic Before Ceremony

The center of gravity is ethical and scholarly, not ritualistic. The texts repeatedly insist on **modesty, charity**, and **useful knowledge**. Where ritual appears (especially in *The Chymical Wedding*), it serves as a **teaching theater**—a way to compress many lessons into one unforgettable sequence.

3) Invisible College Dynamics

By the mid-seventeenth century, Europe was full of correspondence clubs: exchange boxes of specimens, letter-journals of experiments, "experiences" held before witnesses—all the preconditions for modern scientific societies. The Rosicrucian program did not create this alone, but it **accelerated** the pattern by giving it a compelling **mythic frame** that was Christian, reformist, and exciting.

Alchemy Without the Fog: What the Laboratory Meant

Forget the cartoon of alchemy as treasure-hunting for gold. In the Rosicrucian context, alchemy is a **method**:

- **Observation** replaces rote authority.

- **Record-keeping** replaces miracle stories.

TIMELINE AT A GLANCE

- *Late 1400s: Mythic window given in Chymical Wedding (1459) anchors the backstory.*
- *1614–1616: The three Rosicrucian texts appear and circulate.*
- *1610s–1620s: "Rosicrucian furore"—pamphlets pro and con; reading circles; courtly and academic intrigue.*
- *1620s–1660s: Ideas leak into early scientific clubs, reforming pietist groups, and court laboratories; the myth keeps re-seeding itself.*
- *19th–20th centuries: Revivals rebrand the myth for new audiences, often adding rites and bureaucratic structures the original manifestos never specified.*

- **Process** (calcination, dissolution, coagulation, etc.) replaces guesswork.

- **Analogy** is not laziness; it is a way to design experiments that test whether the same pattern holds at different scales.

And the truly radical claim: **character matters**. A vain, greedy practitioner will misread nature and harm patients. A charitable, disciplined one will see what others miss.

The *Chymical Wedding*: The User Manual in Disguise

Why is this strange allegory part of the package? Because it is a **user manual** wearing carnival clothes. Its processions, trials, and surgeries instruct the reader in **attention, proportion,** and **humor** (yes, humor—it guards against fanaticism). It trains you to:

- Weigh claims precisely (the text is full of measurements).

- Keep counsel (the protagonist fails when he brags).

- Bear ambiguity without paralysis (scenes intentionally resist single meanings).

- Prefer **service** to **status** (the "marriage" is the union of opposites for the common good, not a personal coronation).

Myths, Facts, and the Line Between Them

It's useful to sort into three layers:

- **Documented Facts:** The pamphlets exist; their publication dates and reprints are known; the reactions in letters and tracts are preserved; the allegorical novel was certainly penned by a razor-sharp Lutheran humanist with a taste for satire and reform.

- **Reasonable Inferences:** A small circle crafted the program; the authors used anonymity strategically; a confessional (Protestant) reformist ethic frames the project; the myth energized correspondence networks that prefigure later learned societies.

- **Later Accretions:** Elaborate hierarchies, baroque rituals, and sweeping conspiratorial claims belong mostly to **later revivals**. They may be interesting, but they are not what the 1610s manifestos put on the table.

How to Read a Rosicrucian Text Today (and Not Get Lost)

1. **Treat it like an operating manual.** Look for procedures, not just poetry.

2. **Watch the ethics.** When a character fails morally, that often explains the puzzle that follows.

3. **Diagram everything measurable.** Architecture and geometry

> *WHAT TO QUOTE IN A HURRY*
>
> - *"Heal the sick **gratis**."*
> - *"After 120 years I will open."*
> - *"We have the **magia** and **cabala**, but we serve Christ."*
>   *These lines, taken together, summarize charity, timing, and theological alignment.*

are teaching aids.

4. **Translate the virtues.** When you see seven anythings, ask: planets, metals, virtues—how are they mapped?

5. **Ask what problem is being solved.** The target is usually bad medicine, vanity scholarship, or corruption—not "the masses" or "the profane."

Why This Chapter Matters in the Architecture of Hidden Orders

The Rosicrucian manifestos sit exactly at the hinge where **medieval chivalric ideals** (service, honor, vows) meet **early modern technics** (printing, postal networks, experiments). They are the connective tissue between older **orders of knighthood** and newer **societies of inquiry**. They show how a **story** can find a **network**—and how a network can endure precisely because it refuses to be a single building with a single door to kick down.

STRATEGIC LESSON
Narrative can be organizational infrastructure. *Build an ethic and a myth; let print, post, and practice instantiate the "order" everywhere at once.*

Chapter 6

The Freemasons

This chapter follows a trail from medieval stone yards to modern capitals, mapping how a guild of builders became a global fraternity, how its symbols and degrees codified a worldview, why it keeps getting dragged into theories about revolutions, and how one city—Washington, D.C.—became a test case for reading power through plan and stone. We'll keep a clear head. When the evidence is firm, I'll say so. When it's contested, I'll mention. And when the story is exciting but oversold, we'll put it under a hard light.

From cathedral builders to a global fraternity

Start in the cold, with cutters and setters on scaffolds where the wind eats at your hands. "Operative" masons—actual builders—organized themselves to move from site to site, guarding techniques, measuring, and standards. As Europe's guild system faded in the seventeenth and eighteenth centuries, something unlikely happened: the lodges did not simply die; they changed their clientele. Men who weren't stoneworkers were admitted to what became "speculative" Masonry—using the old tools as moral symbols instead of practical kit. Lodges turned into salons with ritual, philanthropy, networking, and debate, pulling in artisans and aristocrats, scientists and soldiers; the variety was a feature, not a bug. Contemporary observers noted how, in the British Isles and on the continent, lodges became fashionable places where people of different classes and politics could meet—some lodges conservative and clerical, others hot with reformist energy.

This new fraternity didn't stay monocultural. One stream—the Scottish Rite—would later be famous for elaborate "higher degrees." Ironically, parts of it grew out of Catholic, royalist, Jacobite circles in exile, a reminder that "Masonic" doesn't mean one thing everywhere, every year.

Alongside the familiar Anglo-American "regular" pattern sat a very different house style in Scandinavia: the Swedish Rite. Housed in Stockholm's Baatska Palace under royal patronage, it presents a consciously Christian, courtly strain of Masonry—aprons and sashes in early degrees, swords and even daggers in others, with some ceremonies staged in purpose-built vaults or sepulchral rooms designed to impress mortality and rebirth on candidates. That rite runs to eleven degrees and, from the eighth onward, clothes initiates in a Templar habit, complete with a ring of lifelong profession and a heraldic identity—an intensity and specificity that set it apart.

What changed when lodges went "speculative"?

The locus of value shifted from stone to symbol. Tools became moral emblems, the lodge became a theater of character formation, and the journeyman's network morphed into a gentleman's society with charity, ritual, and influence. The structure was portable, so it traveled—first across Europe, then across the Atlantic.

Symbols, degrees, and the grammar of a hidden curriculum

Freemasonry is a language of objects. The square and compasses, the level and plumb—each becomes a lesson about fairness, integrity, and upright conduct. Many systems revolve around a dramatic "third degree," built on the allegory of Hiram Abiff, whose ritual death and raising imprint endurance and fidelity. The Swedish Rite goes its own way, skipping Hiram and leaning deeper into Christian-Templar imagery—again, highlighting that there isn't one canonical script so much as a family of related plays.

Ritual space matters. In several traditions, candidates are confronted with memento mori—skulls, coffins, vaulted "crypts"—not as macabre décor but as a pedagogy of limits: you have one life; live it with measure. The effect, especially by candlelight, can be solemn to the point of uncanny.

What about "secret knowledge"? The most widely recognized English-speaking authorities insist that the "secrets" are primarily modes of recognition—passwords, grips, signs—rather than salvation-bearing doctrines. Yet in some branches, claim and counterclaim heat up, particularly where Templar inheritance stories surface. The Swedish Rite's internal myth—linking its authority to a line descending from the last Templar Grand Master's family—shows how powerful the Templar brand remains, even when mainstream Masonry elsewhere keeps theology at arm's length.

There's also the visual vocabulary around the lodge: twin pillars Jachin and Boaz, a "blazing star," an all-seeing eye—the same ideas that spill into architecture and civic monuments. Some Masonic museums of Masonry put these subjects on display, for better or worse; one Austrian exhibit even pushed a controversial triple-faced "Architect of the Universe" image that shows how quickly a symbol can slide into provocation once it leaves ritual context.

Alleged ties to revolutions: smoke, fire, and stage fog

Here's the problem in one sentence: Freemasonry has been used by very different groups for very different ends. That's why historians argue past each other. Some lodges in 18th-century Europe were crucibles of radical talk. Others were explicitly clerical or royalist in tone. Membership lists, over time, run the spectrum from Joseph de Maistre to Giuseppe Garibaldi—from Mozart to Count Basie, Gerald Ford to Duke Ellington. The fraternity's scale and heterogeneity make a single political label a stretch.

France is the easiest case to watch because the Grand Orient of France is overtly political by design—secularist, sometimes militantly so, and historically entwined with currents on the left. Marching in regalia at street protests? Yes, that has happened in the Grand Orient world. In the 20th century, it had prominent members who moved in and out of power and scandal—proof that Masonry could be a vehicle for action, not just allegory. Anglo-American "regular" Masonry doesn't recognize the Grand Orient as regular, which underscores the internal family feud over religion and politics.

Italy provides a darker parable. In the 1980s, the clandestine P2 lodge—"Propaganda Due"—surfaced amid allegations of political plots, corruption, and even murder investigations. One high-profile banker was found dead under London's Blackfriars Bridge, and the P2 membership lists read like a who's who of the Italian establishment. To be clear: P2 was a rogue lodge and not representative—but it showed how the Masonic label could be repurposed for power games that had nothing to do with moral self-improvement.

Then there are the dueling anecdotes that make sweeping generalizations risky. Chile's Salvador Allende wore a Masonic apron; his nemesis, Augusto Pinochet, also joined a lodge as a young officer. If Masonry were a simple predictor of politics, those two facts would not coexist. They do.

Reading politics into Masonry without getting lost

Ask three grounding questions: Which obedience or rite is in play? Which decade are we talking about? Is the "Masonic" group formal and recognized—or improvised and clandestine (as with P2)? Those filters cut through the fog.

Family Tree of Masonic Obediences

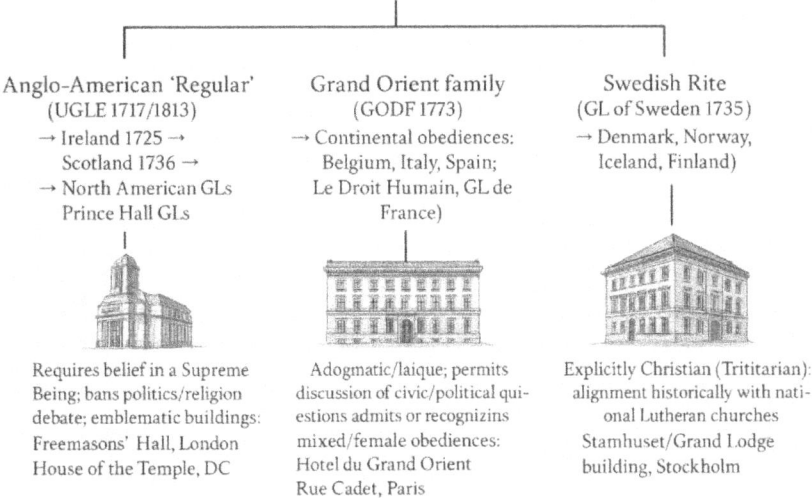

Anglo-American 'Regular' (UGLE 1717/1813)	Grand Orient family (GODF 1773)	Swedish Rite (GL of Sweden 1735)
→ Ireland 1725 → Scotland 1736 → North American GLs Prince Hall GLs	→ Continental obediences: Belgium, Italy, Spain; Le Droit Humain, GL de France)	→ Denmark, Norway, Iceland, Finland)
Requires belief in a Supreme Being; bans politics/religion debate; emblematic buildings: Freemasons' Hall, London House of the Temple, DC	Adogmatic/laique; permits discussion of civic/political qui-estions admits or recognizins mixed/female obediences: Hotel du Grand Orient Rue Cadet, Paris	Explicitly Christian (Trititarian): alignment historically with nati-onal Lutheran churches Stamhuset/Grand Lodge building, Stockholm

Case Study: Washington, D.C., and the "Masonic city plan"

Washington, D.C., is where symbolic reading collides with municipal reality. The things you can touch are not controversial. A short walk up 16th Street NW brings you to the House of the Temple, the headquarters of the Scottish Rite's Supreme Council (Southern Jurisdiction). Designed by John Russell Pope—who also gave the U.S. its Jefferson Memorial—the building is a deliberate temple form, a literal house for speculative art. It is also a mausoleum: the remains of Albert Pike, a central 19th-century figure in the Rite, are entombed there. That's not a rumor; it's on the building's own tour narrative and in standard architectural accounts.

So here's what's **documented** and safe to say:

- Washington, D.C., hosts major Masonic institutions and monuments; the House of the Temple is among the most architecturally explicit.
- Early American elites included many Masons—part of the broader 18th-century transatlantic fraternity culture. (You'll see Benjamin Franklin across that landscape repeatedly.)

Now to the **contested** readings. An entire sub-genre of urban symbolism argues that Washington's plan encodes Masonic geometry: pentagrams in the avenues, the "blazing star" mirrored on the ground, axial alignments with celestial bodies, and the Washington Monument framed as a modern obelisk in a Hermetic composition. Writers in this tradition have linked the city's ritual life to "cornerstone ceremonies," to the idea of "raising" the city, and even to star-sightings—Sirius, Venus—mapped against avenues and pentagons. The thesis is seductive, and it sits inside a larger body of work that connects Cairo, Paris, New York, and Washington through Egypto-Hermetic motifs and revolutionary epochs.

A sober way to read the evidence:

1. **Masonic presence in ceremonial life?** Yes—cornerstone layings, processions, dedications, fraternal attendance are part of American public ritual culture in the 18th–19th centuries.

2. **Pope's classicism at the House of the Temple?** Unambiguous. He intentionally used temple archetypes and a stepped-pyramid massing, so the allusion is built in.

3. **Citywide, intention vs. pareidolia?** It's easy to trace stars and compasses onto any baroque plan with diagonals. If you draw enough lines, you'll see what you're looking for. The discipline is to separate design intent from retrospective pattern-finding. The D.C. plan has French-baroque DNA; Masonic overlays may exist in specific rituals and buildings, but treating the whole map as a cipher demands stronger documentary proof than has usually been offered.

The fraternity's internal paradoxes

Spend time in the archives and you meet two Freemasonries at once. One is civically minded and pragmatic—fundraisers, hospital builders, scholarship endowers. The other is esoteric, comfortable with mythic backstories and long genealogies of symbol. Both live in the same house and sometimes share the same members. That's why you can have—

How to interrogate a "Masonic city" claim

Work from documents outward: (a) surviving drawings and letters from planners/architects; (b) contemporary newspaper accounts of ceremonies; (c) the building program of Masonic bodies living in the city. Treat star-maps and geometric overlays as hypotheses, not conclusions, unless they line up with paper trails.

---

within the same century—lodges that are essentially gentlemen's clubs, and lodges that function as schools of ritual philosophy.

Sweden's high-church royalist model, for example, claims inheritance from the Knights Templar through an internal line of transmission, complete with the Essene and Melchizedek motifs. That claim is controversial and not shared by mainstream Anglo-American bodies. Scholarly work on Templar "survivals" cautions that many 18th-century Templar claims were invented by imaginative system-builders on the German scene and then migrated into later rites. In other words, the mythos is part of Masonry's history—but so is the critique of it.

Revolutions, republics, and reaction: the longer arc

If you look across the long eighteenth and nineteenth centuries, Masonry shows up near the flashpoints not because it puppeteers them but because it networked the sort of people who made history—printers, officers, lawyers, scientists, nobles out of favor and on the make. In France, its radical lodges contributed to the political culture that made the Revolution conceivable; later, Napoleon's imperial theater co-opted and reshaped symbolic capital with a genius for spectacle. In Italy, Garibaldi moved through both lodges and battlefields, enlisting the symbolism of chivalry for a national purpose.

Templar inheritance: what's myth, what's method

Eighteenth-century innovators often grafted Templar legends onto lodge systems to add gravitas. In some places (e.g., the Swedish Rite) that graft became foundational myth. Understanding the fraternity means holding the myth and the minutes together and seeing how each has shaped practice.

In the Americas, transatlantic fraternals—Masonic and otherwise—helped glue elites across colonies and capitals. These are not smoking guns; they're infrastructure: meeting rooms, common rituals, trust built by shared oaths—soft power before the term existed.

The flip side is easy to forget: Masonry also incubated reaction. Royalist rites, churchmen in aprons, princes presiding as patrons—those are as real as the reform clubs. A single fraternity contained the nerve endings of different Europes at once. That's why the story refuses to resolve into "freedom fighters vs. tyrants." It was both—depending on the street, the year, and the obedience.

Washington, revisited: monuments as arguments.

Circle back to the capital and walk it like a dossier. The Washington Monument is an obelisk—Egyptian in inspiration and modern in execution—framed by a city plan that invites symbolic readings. It is fair to say that, since the nineteenth century, Americans have been comfortable clothing civic ideals in classical dress: domes from Rome, columns from Greece, and, yes, obelisks to signal timelessness and aspiration. Those are not secrets; they're a public grammar. Writers who see Hermetic or stellar alignments often extend that grammar, reading star-paths and "blazing stars" into the avenues. The phrases they use—"raising" a city, "cornerstones," "blazing stars"—are undeniably Masonic in tone. The burden of proof is to connect the dots between phrase and plan with documented intention. That's where strong claims are made or broken.

Inside the House of the Temple, meanwhile, you can watch how architecture and rite co-author meaning. Pope's monumental massing makes even a mundane weekday feel ceremonial. The temple that teaches symbol is also a building that performs it; Pike's tomb on site underlines that the fraternity writes its memory into stone.

Edges and outliers: when the label gets misused

Every large banner attracts opportunists. That's why the P2 scandal matters: it demonstrates how a "Masonic" style and structure can be hijacked by actors whose aims are nakedly political or criminal. The Grand Orient's street-march tradition shows, in the opposite direction, a body that embraces politics openly. Neither case defines "Freemasonry" in total; both warn you not to generalize from a fragment.

And sometimes the label simply marks proximity to power. Museums and lodges showcase artifacts that stray into the sensational—like the triple-faced "Architect of the Universe" in Austria—because the line between esoteric symbol and public misunderstanding is thin. It pays to read with context.

A short, hard list of what we can actually say

- **Origins:** The fraternity emerges from late guild culture as "speculative" lodges absorb non-operatives; the mix of classes and ideologies is a feature from the start.

- **Diversity:** Different obediences pull in different directions—the Swedish Rite is royalist and Christian-mystical; the Grand Orient of France is secularist and politically expressive; Anglo-American "regular" Masonry stakes a middle line.

- **Symbols/Degrees:** Hiram for many; Templar motifs for some; recognition signs are the "secrets" in the mainstream; ritual space is designed to transform the candidate's imagination.

- **Politics:** Influence is often infrastructural—networks, rooms, trust. It can tilt radical or reactionary depending on place and period; scandals like P2 are outliers but real.

- **Washington, D.C.:** The presence of Masonic buildings and ceremonies is documented; citywide esoteric readings are debated and require strong, document-based proof.

Tools for the reader moving forward

If you want to keep your footing in this terrain, adopt three habits.

First, contextualize rites. Never assume what you've read about an English lodge fits a Swedish chapter room. The degree structure, the theology, even the garments can be different.

Second, test political claims with mundane paper. Who signed the charter? Who paid the rent? Which newspapers covered the ceremony? Who was photographed wearing what apron? The ordinary trail usually outlives the myth.

Third, treat symbolism as additive, not dispositive. Obelisks, stars, and pillars—these are public-facing, widely used languages in the 18th–20th centuries. Masonic and non-Masonic patrons spoke to them. If a city wears classical clothes, that isn't proof of a hidden hand; it's evidence of a shared architectural vocabulary.

The Freemasons are easiest to caricature and hardest to pin down because they sit where myth and civic life touch. Their buildings make arguments; their rituals turn tools into morals; their networks, at times, have mattered. The fraternity has sheltered conservatives and radicals, churchmen and freethinkers, philanthropists and the occasional plotter. That contradiction is not a flaw in the record; it is the record.

Washington, D.C., remains a living lab: a city whose visible Masonic stones invite invisible readings. Some of those readings hold up; others look like lines drawn after the fact. The safe bet is to keep your eye on documents and your feet on the pavement. Where you can stand and read a cornerstone, do it. Where a temple declares itself, take it seriously on its own terms. Where patterns multiply without paper, mark them as interesting—and keep walking.

Part III: Modern Occult Orders and Conspiratorial Societies

Chapter 7: Illuminati: Myth and Reality

You already know the word. It pops up in lyrics, comment sections, late-night podcasts, and the nervous laughter of friends who half-believe there's a hidden script behind everything. "The Illuminati." Few labels have done more cultural work with less hard evidence. In this chapter, we open the file, page through what can be documented, and separate durable facts from elastic folklore. You'll see how a small, very specific Enlightenment club in Bavaria went from a regional controversy to the all-purpose explanation for revolutions, recessions, and celebrity hand signs.

We're going to do three things, thoroughly and without theatrics:

1. Reconstruct the real Bavarian Illuminati—who founded it, what it tried to do, and why it was suppressed.

2. Track how the name "Illuminati" metastasized into the most persistent conspiracy story on Earth.

3. Put a famous claim under the microscope: alleged Illuminati manipulation of the French Revolution.

The Bavarian Illuminati: Origin vs. Modern Legend

The setting: Bavaria in the age of reforms and censors

Picture a compact, Catholic state in the Holy Roman Empire in the late 1700s. Universities are still policed by church faculty; the printing press is watched; guilds and privileges knit everyday life into tight patterns. Yet new ideas—rationalism, natural rights, critical scholarship—are in the air, carried by books, Masonic lodges, and restless students.

Into that air, on May 1, 1776, a law professor in Ingolstadt launched a project with an audaciously simple premise: if you can cultivate better people, you can get a better polity. He did not invent something magical; he organized something managerial—an order, with rules, degrees, reading lists, and a secretive style designed to protect members and sharpen their discipline.

Core goal (stripped of later mythology): recruit promising minds, train them in reason and ethics, link them across professions, and—quietly—steer public life toward Enlightenment reforms. The secrecy wasn't for theatrical occultism; it was a shield against conservative authorities and an attention-focusing device for members.

What it actually was

- **Structure:** A small, tiered fraternity with "student" grades and "leadership" grades. Advancement required study, writing, and mentorship, not mystical initiation.

- **Method:** Work through existing networks—especially Masonic lodges—by enrolling members who already valued discretion and mutual aid.

- **Curriculum:** Philosophy, moral improvement, anti-superstition argumentation, and practical politics.

- **Aesthetics:** Pseudonyms, coded correspondence, and classical references gave it a cloak-and-dagger feel, but the content was more "seminar" than "seance."

Why secrecy at all?

Secrecy served three functions:

1. **Safety.** Criticizing church and throne—even mildly—was risky in Bavarian circles.

2. **Selective pressure.** Not everyone will read a long tract and write a commentary for advancement unless they are truly committed.

3. **Signal.** A closed door suggests something important is happening; it also reduces performative speech and encourages candor.

Growth, friction, and the decisive clash

Recruitment worked best through people who already had organizing talent. One such organizer modernized the order's procedures, standardized degrees, and negotiated with Masonic lodges to expand the footprint. With growth came predictable problems: loose talk, petty rivalries, and letters that—if seized—would look far more dangerous when ripped from context.

Then the state turned its head. In the early 1780s, Bavaria's ruler issued edicts curbing secret societies. The order, already on the radar, became a priority: house searches, seized correspondence, and publicized extracts portraying it as a subversive syndicate. Leaders went to ground. The order disintegrated under pressure, legal terror, and the fear that any friend might be an informant.

Key Dates at a Glance

- *May 1, 1776: Founding in Ingolstadt.*
- *Early 1780s: Expansion through lodge networks.*
- *1784–1785: Bavarian edicts banning secret associations; raids and arrests follow.*
- *1786–1787: Seized papers are printed to discredit the order.*
- *By 1787: Organization effectively defunct.*

Real scale, real limits

Membership fluctuated and was always smaller than later legends suggest. We're talking about a few hundred to perhaps a couple thousand names across German lands, not a continent-spanning shadow government. Their influence was episodic and mostly local— nudges inside university, court, and lodge circles.

Puncturing the modern myths—calmly

Myth 1: Timeless puppet-masters

Reality: A short-lived Enlightenment network, dissolved years before the French Revolution reached full speed.

Myth 2: Occult ritualists

Reality: Devotion to reason and reform, not ceremonial magic. Secrecy ≠ sorcery.

Myth 3: The Eye in the Pyramid

Reality: The "All-Seeing Eye" has older Christian and Masonic antecedents and appears in various contexts. There's no credible pipeline from a small Bavarian club to every version of that symbol around the world.

Myth 4: The One Organization Behind Everything

Reality: Political outcomes have multiple, often contradictory drivers. Folding complexity into a single villain is psychologically satisfying— and historically misleading.

How "Illuminati" Became the Most Enduring Conspiracy

The order died; the label lived. Understanding why means tracing how names—and anxieties—travel.

Step 1: The perfect villain enters the bookshelf

When Bavaria printed selected confiscated letters for public consumption, they served a double purpose: to justify the crackdown and terrify readers. Soon, writers hostile to the upheavals of the late 18th century discovered they could turn a local club into a universal culprit. The word "Illuminati" became a rhetorical knuckle-duster— less a documented group than an accusation that your opponent is secretly coordinating society's unravelling.

How this works psychologically: complex change feels chaotic; a single hidden cause promises order. If there's a mastermind, there's a plan; if there's a plan, there's meaning. That cognitive relief is intoxicating.

Step 2: The pamphlet becomes a template

Nineteenth-century polemicists learned to weaponize secret-society tropes: anonymous cells, initiation oaths, staged "revelations." In the United States, anti-Masonic agitation after a sensational disappearance taught activists that the mere rumor of hidden oaths could mobilize

---

Why the Name Stuck

• *Memorable branding: "Illuminati" sounds dramatic, slightly sacrilegious, and easy to say.*
• *Moral clarity: It turns messy history into battle lines: "us" vs. "the manipulators."*
• *Reusability: You can paste it onto any era's anxieties— revolutions, recessions, pop culture—without changing the script.*
• *Evidence-proofing: Any lack of proof can be framed as proof of how powerful the conspirators are.*

---

voters. The exact facts mattered less than the feeling that elites were whispering behind closed doors.

"Illuminati," by now, had floated free from its Bavarian roots. It could mean "any clandestine manipulator." If a modern banker, a revolutionary, a journalist, or a novelist made you uneasy, you had a word.

Step 3: Pop culture polishes the myth

Twentieth-century thrillers and twenty-first-century internet culture added new layers: hieroglyphic symbols on currency, celebrity "signals," and cinematic plots where a small cabal micromanages centuries. The internet then did what it does best: turned fragments into a self-updating mythos. The label survives because it's modular, memetic, and genuinely entertaining.

Step 4: The word becomes a catch-all

By now, accusing someone of being "Illuminati" requires little content. It's an all-weather allegation: if an event seems too tidy, too lucky, or simply unwelcome, blame the cabal. This elasticity is precisely why the story endures: it's a plot device as much as a plot.

Case Study: The French Revolution and "Illuminati Infiltration"

Let's test the loudest claim. Did the Bavarian Illuminati seed the Jacobin Clubs and steer the French Revolution?

What the claim says

The short version: "Agents of the Illuminati penetrated Parisian Masonry before 1789, recruited key revolutionaries, and guided the overthrow of monarchy, church, and property."

It's a compelling script. It also runs into a brick wall of timing, logistics, and documentary silence.

The historical clock

- The Bavarian organization was harassed and legally strangled in 1784–1785.

- Its correspondence is seized and published in 1786–1787, scattering members and burning networks.

- The French Revolution broke out in 1789, with the most radical institutional changes happening from 1792–1794.

That's not a clean hand-off; it's a gap. A dissolved German circle would have needed not just to survive, but to re-cross borders, rebuild cells in a hostile foreign environment, and then out-organize every faction in Paris—while leaving almost no paper trail even as French politics spewed pamphlets and police reports by the mile.

The Parisian ecosystem before 1789

Long before anyone in Paris ever muttered "Illuminati," the city swarmed with clubs, salons, lodges, reading rooms, and debating societies. Reformist nobles, lawyers, army officers, and middle-class professionals were already talking about debt crises, grain shortages, court corruption, venal offices, and constitutional fixes. There were homegrown traditions of radical thought—physiocrats, philosophes, pamphleteers—plus a fiscal meltdown that would have blown the roof off any system.

Put more bluntly, tinder was piled high in France for decades. You don't need a German match to explain the blaze.

What Would Real Infiltration Evidence Look Like?

- *Letters between named Bavarian operatives and named Parisian club leaders planning tactics.*
- *Consistent funding trails linking German paymasters to French agitators.*
- *Arrest records or interrogations acknowledging a directive relationship.*
- *Internal minutes using Bavarian degree language or code names.*
- *We don't have this. We have later accusations and speculative chains, not operational documents.*

The Bode problem (and why it doesn't rescue the theory)

One name often surfaces: a capable German organizer who traveled, met French brethren, and discussed reformist ideas in the late 1780s. His itinerary and interests are not in serious doubt. The leap comes when writers turn a set of lodge conversations into an invisible command network. Enthusiastic exchanges between reformers are not the same thing as a chain of command—especially when the Germans' home organization had been wrecked by arrests and public scandal.

The Jacobins were a French creation, with French dynamics

The core revolutionary clubs grew out of French political conditions: provincial grievances, legal-professional cultures, and intense competition among factions within Paris itself. Their discipline and ferocity were shaped by wartime emergencies and purges, not by a decade-old reading society from Bavaria.

Why the accusation thrived anyway

It's narratively irresistible to believe that a single secret order "caused" the Revolution. It reallocates blame from a nation's longstanding structural problems—debt, privilege, famine responses, political mismanagement—to a handful of villains. It also flatters the counter-revolutionary reader: if only the cabal had been stopped, order would have returned. Reality is less tidy: France cracked under the weight of its own contradictions.

The Afterlife of a Name

Once the French case became famous, the template was reusable: whenever a rapid change felt destabilizing, "Illuminati" could be stamped on it. The reason is simple: the label functions like a master key. It opens any locked door in the imagination—because it pretends those doors all have the same lock.

That's not how history works. But it is how myths work.

Why the story refuses to die

1. **It's simple.** A small group → big outcomes.

2. **It's dramatic.** Secret oaths and coded letters are great theater.

3. **It's flexible.** It absorbs new enemies—bankers today, technologists tomorrow—without changing its skeleton.

4. **It's social.** Believing it can bond you to a community that "knows what's really going on."

ONE LABEL, MANY FEARS

Why This Matters

You might ask: if the Illuminati, as a specific Bavarian order, were small and short-lived, and if the modern usage is a cultural meme more than a historical fact, why spend a whole chapter on it?

Because the label shapes how people think about power. When every outcome is chalked up to a hidden omnipotence, we stop asking the harder questions—about institutions, incentives, and the boring, daily machinery that actually moves societies. "Illuminati" is the story we reach for when complexity feels unbearable. Understanding the gap between the club and the myth gives us a way to keep our footing.

And there's a second gain: once you stop treating "Illuminati" as a master key, you can start mapping real, documented hidden orders—some benign, some predatory—on their own terms. You'll see precisely where secrecy aids learning, where it deters accountability, and where it becomes a mask for criminality. You'll also notice how many "secret" places are simply private—banks, clubs, sanctuaries—shielded not by occult force but by laws, customs, and architecture.

The Productive Use of Secrecy

- *Incubation: New ideas need quiet space before public debate.*
- *Protection: Dissenters in authoritarian settings require cover.*
- *Coordination: Small, high-trust groups can act faster than committees.*

The danger appears when secrecy becomes a substitute for legitimacy, not a tool to earn it.

A Straight Answer to the Big Three

1) The Bavarian Illuminati—origin vs. legend

A reformist, Enlightenment-era order founded in 1776 in Bavaria used secrecy as a practical tool, grew modestly through lodge networks, and was dissolved by legal force by 1787. It was not an occult cabal or an ancient survival; it was a short-run, documentable organization with human flaws.

2) Why the Illuminati became the enduring conspiracy

Its confiscated papers and the anxieties of an age created irresistible copy. Later writers found the brand so handy that they stapled it to every anxiety, and popular media did the rest, turning a localized club into a universal bogeyman.

3) French Revolution infiltration theories

The timeline doesn't fit, the mechanisms aren't demonstrated, and the Revolution had ample local fuel. Cross-border conversations existed; command-level infiltration is not supported by operational evidence.

Field Notes: People, Places, Papers

This section gathers the recurring nouns you'll meet, framed briefly so you can keep the landscape straight as you read more widely.

Ingolstadt: University town where the order began.

Lodges: Not a synonym for "Illuminati," but the network through which recruitment often ran.

Bavarian edicts (1784–1785): Legal tools that criminalized secret associations, triggering raids.

Seized papers (mid-1780s): Printed by the authorities to discredit the order; later polemicists mined them selectively.

Parisian clubs (1789 onward): Homegrown political engines; they fought one another fiercely and changed shape under war pressure.

What Survives, and What Doesn't

Of the Bavarian project, what survives are:

- **Documents:** administrative rules, correspondence, and reading assignments.

- **Reputation:** inflated by adversaries and romancers.

- **Lessons:** about how small, disciplined groups can punch above their weight until the state seriously notices them.

What does not survive:

- **Continuity:** No credible, unbroken organizational chain runs from Ingolstadt to modern politics.

- **Occult power:** The drama is in the pamphlets, not in the physics.

- **Omnipotence:** A network that could be shattered by local police was never the universal master of events.

Practical Takeaways for the Reader-Investigator

You're part of the investigation now. Here's how to stay sharp when the next headline or thread waves the word "Illuminati" in your face.

- **Ask for the boring details.** Who met? Where? How often? Who paid?

- **Follow the paper.** The bigger the alleged influence, the more it should leave receipts—money, messages, minutes.

- **Cross-examine the timeline.** If you need a time machine to make the claim work, the claim doesn't work.

- **Compare alternative causes.** Economics, institutions, and personalities explain more than secret councils do.

- **Treat symbols as art, not evidence.** An eye or a triangle is a canvas. Meaning depends on context, not a universal decoder ring.

The Illuminati story endures because it delivers what many of us secretly want: a single, dramatic explanation that ties together the terrifying mess of history. The real story is smaller and, in an oddly satisfying way, more human—a group of idealists who tried to hack institutional change with study circles and discreet networking, only to run into the hard edges of a cautious state and the shrapnel of their own ambition.

What their legend leaves us is a cognitive trap and a cultural toy. What their reality leaves us is a case study in how ideas travel, how secrecy works, and how easily our hunger for pattern can outrun the evidence. Keep your curiosity; it's your best instrument. Couple it with discipline, and you'll see more clearly through the fog—no matter how many eyes and pyramids stare back from the margins.

Chapter 8

Skull and Bones and the American Elite

You don't break into Skull and Bones; you get invited, and you arrive five minutes early—or rather, five minutes late everywhere else. Inside the windowless tomb at 64 High Street in New Haven, even the clocks run on their own schedule, a subtle declaration that "our time" is not the same as everyone else's.

Bones is a Yale senior society, the oldest and most myth-saturated of the set. Only fifteen students are "tapped" each spring, a tiny intake that keeps the network tight and the aura concentrated. Across generations, that small annual class has yielded an outsized cascade of bankers, cabinet officials, philanthropists, judges, media figures, executives, and—famously—presidents.

The society's peculiar mix of ritual theater, enforced intimacy, and lifetime fraternity is not an accident. It's a machine built for conversion: turning talented undergraduates into bonded peers who, upon graduation, scatter into the choke points of American power yet remain reachable by a shared code. What follows is an investigative, document-driven walk-through that machine—how it formed, what it does, and what it doesn't do—with a close look at the Bush family as a test case.

The Yale Society That Shaped Presidents and Bankers

Skull and Bones is the flagship among Yale's "senior societies," a cluster of invitation-only groups with permanent halls—"tombs" in Yale parlance—where members meet twice weekly through senior year. In order of traditional precedence, the marquee list includes Skull and Bones, Scroll and Key, Wolf's Head, Berzelius, Book and Snake, St. Elmo, Elihu, Manuscript, and Mace and Chain. Elihu alone brands itself "nonsecret." All now admit women, a shift that roiled some groups—Bones most of all—when coeducation forced change onto a deliberately unchanging world.

Bonesmen and their rivals built an entire micro-city of secrecy in downtown New Haven: the Greco-Egyptian mass of the Bones tomb at 64 High Street; the Moorish fantasia of Scroll and Key at 444 College Street; and the high-walled Cotswold manor of Wolf's Head on York Street, the latter designed by Bertram Goodhue and paid for by oil heir Edward Harkness.

Inside Bones, you enter a ritual world with rules that are simple, strange, and memorable: do not bring metal to initiation (arrive symbolically "penniless"); learn and use a new, secret name; refer to non-members as "Barbarians"; look up—the sanctuary ceiling is a star-field, a classic initiatic device symbolizing passage into a new realm. The "Inner Temple," also called Room 322, is the heart of the space. And then there's the society's signature quirk: all tomb clocks are set five minutes ahead—"Bones time."

Rituals, Secrecy, and the Psychology of Bonding

Bones borrows broadly from the "initiatic" repertoire—symbolic poverty, new identity, liminality—but executes it with an intentionally jarring tone. Initiation is loud and disorienting; the goal is to mark a

---

What Makes Bones Different (In a Nutshell)

- *Annual intake capped at 15 students; lifetime membership.*
- *Meetings in a permanent tomb at 64 High Street (New Haven).*
- *Inner Temple/Room 322 as ritual core; clocks run on "Bones time."*
- *Initiates arrive with no metal; all members adopt secret names; outsiders are "Barbarians."*

hard break with the ordinary and to weld a new cohort quickly. One practice that surfaces in reliable accounts: structured sessions in which members disclose intimate life histories—including sexual histories—to the group. Whether you view that as lurid or therapeutic, it's deliberate: forced candor collapses façades and creates a powerful sense of "us."

While Bones guards its internal mythos, its legal face is surprisingly mundane. The society operates through a charitable entity—historically the Russell Trust Association, now RTA Incorporated—that files public paperwork describing its mission in bland terms: "structured programs of intellectual inquiry, sensitivity training and personal development," recently on topics like homeland security, corporate governance, and international relations. The phrasing may sound corporate, but it confirms a core point: behind the mystique, the weekly rhythm is talk—guided, candid, peer-to-peer talk.

The "Bones Time" Principle
Set the clocks five minutes ahead; keep the doorways right on time. The message is simple: inside, you live on our cadence; outside, the world waits. A tiny ritual, a daily reminder.

Five Past in Room 322

Rivals and the Ecosystem Around Bones

Bones exist inside a competitive ecosystem. Scroll and Key, housed in an ornate Moorish tomb, maintains its own mystique and legal shell (Kingsley Trust Association). Its alumni list reads like a transatlantic address book—from diplomats and publishers to composers and cultural figures—and members cap meetings with a midnight song outside the tomb door. Wolf's Head, long ranked third, boasts two architecturally distinguished tombs and a venerable alumni roster. Manuscript, Elihu, Book and Snake, and others run on similar weekly cadences, swapping ritual vocabulary but preserving the same formula: a year of intense storytelling, debate, and bonding.

Influence, Not Omnipotence: How the Network Works

The society has no public platform and no published creed; it has alumni. That's the point. When you select fifteen ambitious students a year for nearly two centuries, the resulting network will appear in high places. Media coverage often name-checks the most visible pairings—both Presidents Bush, Senator John Kerry—then forgets the equally instructive roster: FedEx founder Fred Smith, private-equity cofounder Stephen Schwarzman, humorist Christopher Buckley, and many others in finance, law, media, academia, and public service.

Influence here is not a conspiracy board with a red string; it's path dependence. Members leave Yale already socialized to think aloud with peers who challenge them, then enter feeder firms and agencies that prize the same confidence, discretion, and decisiveness. The "Bones effect" is less about pulling levers in secret and more about having a Rolodex of people you trust when hard decisions come fast.

Confirmed, Probable, and Folkloric: Sorting Bones Lore

Confirmed elements: tiny intake; permanent tomb; initiatic devices (no metal, secret names, "Bones time," starry ceiling); discussion-heavy

---

What "Influence" Looks Like in Practice
- *A phone answered on the first ring by someone you met in a star-painted room.*
- *A reference that bypasses HR and lands on a managing partner's desk.*
- *A policy memo read with extra care because you recognize the name.*

That's not mind control. It's social capital—dense, tested, and immediately convertible.

program; a charitable shell (RTA Inc.) describing intellectual and personal-development aims; a tradition of not talking to outsiders.

Probable elements: a historically Germanic aesthetic and memorabilia in the tomb; an Illuminist-style print bearing a German verse about equality in death; a fascination with memento mori across rooms and props. That imagery is consistent with 19th-century Masonic and Catholic symbolism and with the era's taste for mortality reminders; it doesn't prove a living link to any continental order.

Folklore: elaborate claims about command-and-control over politics or markets don't match the structure you actually see—fifteen undergraduates per year, a discussion curriculum, and a diaspora of alumni. The network is real; the world-domination plotline isn't necessary to explain the outcomes.

From the Tomb to Wall Street and Washington

If you want to see how a small Yale society leaves fingerprints on American institutions, study private partnerships and the old-line banks. Brown Brothers Harriman—famously clubby, resolutely private, and once at 59 Wall Street—counted Prescott Bush (Senator, father and grandfather of presidents) and W. Averell Harriman among its partners. A notable number of partners across eras came from Yale's senior societies, Bones among them, and several later held major government posts. That pattern, more than any dramatic ceremony, explains the "Bones-to-power" pipeline people speculate about.

The firm's prestige also brushed against global finance: Montagu Norman trained at 59 Wall before becoming Governor of the Bank of England, the most consequential central banker of his era. The circle was small, the rooms intimate, and the letters of introduction decisive.

Case Study: The Bush Family and Skull and Bones Ties

The family arc. Senator Prescott Bush sat in the center ring of mid-century finance as a Brown Brothers Harriman partner and a prominent public figure. His son George H. W. Bush (Yale '48) and grandson George W. Bush (Yale '68) both joined Skull and Bones as undergraduates; when the younger Bush ran for a second term in 2004, his opponent John Kerry—also a Bones alumnus—turned the race into a peculiar reunion of New Haven seniors under Klieg lights.

What the record shows. The Bush family's trajectory maps neatly onto the standard routes out of Bones: elite finance (Prescott), national security and energy (George H. W. Bush), statehouse to White House (George W. Bush), with campaign and cabinet staffing that drew heavily on the same schools, firms, clubs, and think tanks. It's tempting to over-read that map. The more accurate lesson is simpler: people who have trained to make fast, confidential decisions together at twenty-one tend to recognize and hire one another at forty-one.

Where a tap likely mattered—and where it didn't. — **Mattered:** initial introductions; early job doors opening; trust transfers across organizations; donors and bundlers returning calls.

— **Didn't:** electoral math; legislative coalitions; foreign policy constraints; market cycles and exogenous shocks. A tomb can produce allies; it can't repeal gravity.

Rituals as Social Technology

Bones' toolkit is best understood as social engineering for cohesion:

- **Symbolic poverty (no metal at initiation):** strips status props and declares equality under the rite.

- **New names:** flatten hierarchy and create a playful, private grammar that keeps the group exclusive without being outwardly hostile.

- **Star-field ceilings and Room 322:** enclose the group in a "second world," signaling that different rules—and confidences—apply here.

- **"Bones time":** a tiny daily friction that keeps members aware of the boundary between inside and out.

- **Confessional sessions:** accelerate trust by swapping curated vulnerability for lifelong discretion.

None of this requires secret levers in Washington. It reliably produces adults who will pick up the phone for each other, and that alone moves money, policy, and careers in a country where informal networks are often faster than formal ones.

After Bones: The Wider Senior-Society Web

Bones' rivals matter because they complicate the monoculture story. Scroll and Key, Manuscript, Book and Snake, Elihu, and Wolf's Head recruit overlapping but distinct cohorts: journalists, investors, artists, future administrators, and wonks. Manuscript drew Jodie Foster and Anderson Cooper; Book and Snake counted a CIA director and a leading scholar among alumni; Wolf's Head maintained its own powerful fraternity in law and public life. That pluralism is why New Haven has produced leaders across ideologies and sectors—and why Bones' influence is real but not monopolistic.

What Changed—and What Didn't

Coeducation, culture wars, and the democratization of admissions forced every senior society to adapt. Bones took its lumps—internal fights over women, public exposés, a flood of wry press. A well-known magazine once rated elite networks and teased Bones for waning "power" but maxed out its scores for secrecy, peculiarity of ritual, and exclusivity—the brand's core signals. Even after bruising reforms, the basic machine kept running: small class, intense bonding, lifetime ties.

The charitable shell's public language also evolved. Where a century ago a society might have shrugged at public explanation, the paperwork now sprinkles modern phrases—"sensitivity training," "corporate governance"—as if to reassure onlookers that what goes on inside is civil and constructive. Read alongside corroborated accounts of practices and space, it is. It's also deliberately not *for* you.

Secrecy as a Force Multiplier

Skull and Bones doesn't "run" America. It trains Americans—some of whom later run things. The society's genius is to compress years of trust-building into a single, ritualized calendar year, then to protect that trust with privacy, shared language, and the memory of nights in a room painted with stars.

For readers of this book, the important lesson is diagnostic. When you encounter any modern "hidden order," ask: What is the intake? What are the rituals really doing? Where do alumni show up? Do documents and addresses match the myth? With Bones, the answers are legible:

- **Intake:** Fifteen.

> ### The Hidden Order Pattern (Reusable Lens)
>
> *Small gate + intensive bonding + ritualized privacy → fast trust → elite placement → iterative reinforcement. Plug this lens into the next chapter's subjects and watch the noise resolve into*

- **Rituals:** Designed to erase status, enforce candor, and create an "elsewhere."

- **Alumni footprint:** Visible across finance, government, and culture, with clear concentrations in relationship-driven institutions like partnership banks.

- **Paper trail:** A charitable shell spelling out a discussion-based program, however antiseptic the phrasing.

Chapter 9

The Occult Revival of the 19th & 20th Centuries

Pull on any one thread in the 19th–20th-century occult revival and you find it stitched into places you might not expect— poetry and painting; party politics and police states; clubrooms and concentration camps. The period gave us new esoteric fraternities with elaborate grade systems and ritual magick; grand theories about hidden masters and ancient races; and a persistent belief that symbols—placed just so—could bend destiny. Some of it was theatre. Some of it was scholarship. And some of it, tragically, became policy.

What follows is a clear, source-driven walk through that terrain—how groups like the Hermetic Order of the Golden Dawn systematized ritual magick; how charismatic operators like Aleister Crowley weaponized charisma into a personal "law"; how esoteric styles and networks bled outward into culture and, at times, into governance; and why the Nazi experiment with myth and ritual at Wewelsburg remains the most chilling case study of occultism merged with state power.

"Occult revival" doesn't mean a single organization directing history. It means many small, sometimes competing groups standardizing ritual practices and mythic frameworks that later seeped into literature, art, alternative religion, and— occasionally—political movements.

The set and setting: why the 1800s were ripe for esotericism

Industrialization dislocated old certainties. Archaeology and philology opened windows onto Egypt, Mesopotamia, and India. Mesmerism and spiritualism flooded parlors. New printing technologies made manuscripts once confined to a few readers widely available. In that weather system, "occult" didn't feel like a fringe—just another research program into mind, meaning, and power.

A few baselines:

- "Ritual magick" in this era meant a disciplined program of symbolic actions, visualizations, invocations, and record-keeping—not stage tricks. Groups borrowed freely from Kabbalah, Renaissance grimoires, Rosicrucian manifestos, and John Dee's angelic (Enochian) materials, then wrapped them in modern organizational charts and exams.

- The social technology of the lodge—oaths, degrees, lectures, regalia—was the engineering chassis. In some places, lodges were civic salons. In others, they were militant. Even critics noticed the reach: you could find Masonic aprons on Latin American presidents of opposing ideologies, a reminder that fraternal forms cut across left-right lines when it came to networking elites.

- Esoteric fellow-travelers sometimes leveraged Masonic ideas as a gateway into "harder" pursuits. The twentieth century's most notorious magician folded lodge insights into his own system, and later popularizers built entire new religions using lodge scaffolding.

The Golden Dawn: laboratory of ritual magick

If the revival had a working classroom, this was it. The Hermetic Order of the Golden Dawn (founded in London in 1888) organized a modular curriculum from disparate sources—Hermetic philosophy, Kabbalah, astrology, tarot, geomancy, and angelic magic—then required members to log results, pass examinations, and advance through graded initiations. The point wasn't blind belief; it was practice and data.

How the engine worked.

A candidate entered a symbolic cosmos: the Tree of Life as a memory palace; pentagram and hexagram rituals to "banish" and "invoke" elemental and planetary forces; skrying in the spirit-vision; pathworking through the 22 Hebrew-letter "paths"; and a constant cycle of ritual, meditation, and journaling. This standardized, "laboratory-like" approach to inner work was the Order's revolution.

What it standardized.

Much of what later generations think of as "ceremonial magic" was codified here: daily banishings and invocations; layered divine names; elemental weapons (wand, cup, sword, pentacle) as anchors for attention and will; and an initiatory map stitched to the Tree of Life. The language of the lodge—grades, passwords, lectures—made complex material teachable.

Fault lines.

Strong minds mean strong quarrels. Factions formed. Claims of authority and secret chiefs led to splintering. Yet even the schisms spread the tech: members carried the curriculum into poetry salons, art studios, occult bookshops, and—eventually—new orders.

Aleister Crowley: from lodge to law

Crowley joined the Golden Dawn in the 1890s, learned its system, fought with its leadership, then founded his own mystical-magical path—Thelema—summed in the infamous line, "Do what thou wilt shall be the whole of the Law." That sentence is often misunderstood. In the Thelemic vocabulary, "will" isn't whim; it's a person's unique, discovered life-task. The system he built took the Golden Dawn's drill, blended it with yoga and tantra, spliced in Enochian elements, and reissued a personal-gnosis-first path with rituals to match.

Why he mattered culturally:

- **Distribution.** Crowley published relentlessly. He turned private lodge techniques into public prints—ritual scripts, meditation methods, commentaries—so the "how-to" escaped closed rooms.

- **Style.** He made occultism a lifestyle brand before marketing language existed for it. The mash-up of Eastern techniques and Western ritual showed later generations how to mix traditions without apology.

- **Spillover.** His work seeded or influenced later groups—directly through students and indirectly through books. In the mid-20th century, a civil servant and lodge member repackaged select lodge ideas into a new, nature-centric religion whose ritual structure echoes lodge forms. That through-line—from lodge to Crowley to new religious movements—is well attested.

How esoteric groups bent culture (and sometimes policy)

You don't need a conspiracy to explain cultural reach when you have (1) coherent symbols, (2) motivated networks, and (3) meeting places. Three channels mattered most.

1) Architecture and civic symbolism.

Fraternal bodies loved buildings that were built of stone. The House of the Temple in Washington, D.C., designed by John Russell Pope (architect of the Jefferson Memorial), became a showpiece of that impulse: an urban temple combining classical language with an esoteric program, and—remarkably—the chosen resting place of a 19th-century esotericist whose voluminous writings long served as a touchstone in one branch of the craft. However people interpret his theology, the fact of his entombment there is uncontested; it anchors the building's cultural story.

2) Elite cross-traffic.

The lodge model appealed to professionals, artists, officers, and politicians across ideologies; one can find heads of state on both left and right who wore aprons at some stage. That doesn't prove a single hidden program. It does explain how ideas, styles, and fashions traveled across sectors quickly. When elites meet regularly under oath, the habit of coordination follows.

3) The arts.

From fin-de-siècle poetry circles to interwar presses, esoteric symbolism bled into headlines and book covers—pentagrams and hexagrams, tarot archetypes, Egyptianizing motifs. Some of this came via Golden Dawn alumni in literature and theatre. Some came via Theosophy and its art-forward offshoots. And by the mid-century, these motifs had become a visual vocabulary that advertising and music could lift without footnotes.

HOUSE OF THE TEMPLE –
Elevation & Cutaway
Washington, D.C., 1915

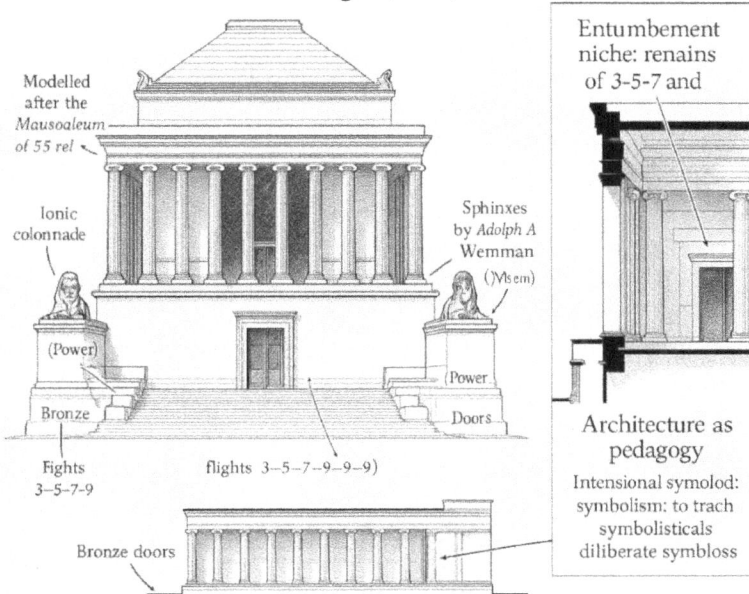

Entumbement niche: renains of 3-5-7 and

Modelled after the *Mausoaleum of 55 rel*

Ionic colonnade

Sphinxes by *Adolph A Wemman* ()Ms em)

(Power)

(Power)

Bronze

Doors

Fights 3–5–7-9

flights 3–5–7–9–9–9)

Bronze doors

Architecture as pedagogy

Intensional symolod: symbolism: to trach symbolisticals diliberate symbloss

Case study — Nazi occultism and the Thule milieu

If you want the dark edge of the revival's political entanglements, you end up in Westphalia, standing over a triangular Renaissance fortress that one of the twentieth century's most infamous bureaucrats tried to turn into the spiritual seat of a new, murderous knighthood.

The scene: Wewelsburg

Wewelsburg Castle—built 1603–1609 for the Prince-Bishop of Paderborn—sits near sites Germans long romanticized (the Teutoburg Forest; Externsteine). In the 1930s, Heinrich Himmler leased it on the cheap and began reshaping it as an ideological center for the SS, grafting a modern police apparatus onto a fantasy of Germanic chivalry. The plan drew on medieval orders and Arthurian imagery, but its core myths were lifted from Nordicist and theosophical speculation, not history.

Inside the North Tower, a marble-inlaid "Black Sun" disk became the visual lodestone of the project; above, an oak table encircled by twelve named chairs provided a stage for a "Round Table" of senior SS. Names and coats of arms were invented to supply prestige that the new "knights" didn't actually possess. At least once, the room was used for high-level briefings, including war planning—an omen of how the costume drama served killing.

The guru and the office

Himmler had an esoteric adviser, Karl Maria Wiligut—an ex-Austrian officer steeped in runic mysticism and personal myth, who designed the SS death's-head ring and celebrated pagan-style rites. His influence helped jump-start the Wewelsburg program; later, the SS research office (Ahnenerbe) took the lead, sending expeditions and underwriting ideological projects. Wiligut himself, dogged by the record of his earlier confinement, slipped from favor before the war's end.

The Ahnenerbe's portfolio veered from folklore and archaeology into outright crank history and pseudoscience—quests for Atlantis and Tibetan "Aryans"—while Wewelsburg hosted torchlit solstice rites, marriages, and invented "baptisms" for SS offspring. The point wasn't harmless cosplay. These rites pressured officers to internalize a replacement morality where loyalty to a race myth trumped conscience.

Blood in the mortar

The Wewelsburg project ran on slave labor from the nearby Niederhagen camp. It wasn't a mass-extermination complex, yet nearly a third of the 3,900 inmates died from starvation, beatings, and overwork between 1940 and 1943; after that, survivors were pushed on to Buchenwald. The "Black Vatican," as the site has been called, thus combined kitsch mythology with real corpses.

In late March 1945, with U.S. armor closing, SS men touched off charges in the southeast tower and let fire do the rest; the North Tower survived, feeding postwar talk of "mystical power," though the prosaic explanation is sturdier construction.

WHAT'S DOCUMENTED VS. WHAT'S SPECULATION

Documented: *lease and renovation budgets; the "Black Sun" floor; the twelve-chair hall; solstice ceremonies; SS marriages; Wiligut's ring design; the adjacent concentration camp supplying forced labor; the 1945 demolition attempt.*
Speculative: *claims of human sacrifice in the crypt; miraculous properties of the tower; elaborate secret rites beyond commemorations—none of which are evidenced in surviving records.*

One macabre loose end: thousands of returned death's-head rings were reportedly hidden in a nearby cave. If the hoard ever existed, it has not been recovered.

The Thule connection—and limits

Long before 1933, Germany swarmed with völkisch and theosophical clubs praising a mythic Aryan past. Circles using the name "Thule" trafficked in Nordicist lore and hosted right-wing activists; their ideas—and occasionally their personnel—overlapped with the nationalist ferment that birthed the early Nazi party. But it's a category error to claim that a single closed lodge "ran" the Reich. What happened instead is simpler and more disturbing: a security boss with a mystical streak built an internal cult, then used it to lubricate mass crime. Even Hitler, who liked shiny trophies such as the famed "Spear of Destiny," rolled his eyes at neo-pagan enthusiasms when they competed with his own cult of will.

Distortions vs. realities: reading the revival with a cold eye

It's easy to get lost in the fog. Here's how to stay oriented.

Mythic framing isn't harmless when the state adopts it. In private, invented coats of arms and ersatz "knightly" rites are cosplay. In a regime, they're moral solvents. Himmler's northern-European myth machine didn't remain a subculture; it refashioned the SS as a priesthood of race. The concentration-camp statistics around Wewelsburg make that tangible.

Fraternal networks explain influence without invoking puppet masters.

A single lodge doesn't move history like a joystick. But when artists, bankers, colonels, and ministers meet weekly under oath, ideas move farther, faster. That's a sociological reality, not a conspiracy theory. The fact that political opponents in South America could both carry lodge memberships in their early careers is a strong clue: the form is a carrier, not the ideology.

Occultism's biggest cultural export was *method*, not dogma.

Daily rituals, visualization routines, graded study, and reflective journaling migrated into everything from psychotherapy and executive coaching to performance training. Crowley's flamboyance grabs headlines; the quiet drills changed lives.

Separating symbol from cause.

You'll see pentagrams and obelisks in capitals. That doesn't prove "control." It usually proves a taste for classical language plus a channel for fraternal donors to leave marks. When a building *does* embed an esoteric program—again, the House of the Temple is a model—there's usually a paper trail and a local story to match.

Frequently misunderstood: three clarifications.

1) "Ritual magick makes people powerful."

It can focus people. It can give them a narrative identity. But power comes from institutions, money, guns, and laws. At Wewelsburg, the rituals followed the police power—not the other way around.

2) "All lodges are occult."

Most are social-civic fraternities with lectures, charity drives, and a taste for symbolism. Some offshoots play deeper with esoteric practice; others don't. One 20th-century American house of the craft even doubles as a museum and shrine, an odd hybrid that shows how public and esoteric can coexist in a single address.

3) "Hitler was the chief occultist."

He liked pageantry and objects that burnished his myth, but often mocked neo-pagan fixations. Himmler was the believer who built a cult inside the state. That distinction matters.

Practical reading list of places and artifacts (as investigative waypoints)

If you're following the trail on the ground:

- **Washington, D.C.—House of the Temple.** A primer in fraternal classicism and how architecture encodes a worldview, including the entombment of a major 19th-century esotericist.

- **Wewelsburg Castle, North Tower.** The "Black Sun" floor, the twelve-chair hall, the crypt below, and the museum exhibits documenting forced labor and the site's role in SS ideology.

- **Dornach, Switzerland—Goetheanum.** Not Nazi-adjacent, but part of the revival's broader landscape of modern esoteric centers, with debates about quasi-Masonic forms.

A sober model of influence

Think of the occult revival as a **toolkit**, a **style**, and a **social web**.

- **Toolkit**: repeatable practices that train attention and story—banishings, invocations, visualizations, pathworkings, journaling.

- **Style**: a taste for layered symbols (Egyptian, Hermetic, Kabbalistic), for ritual theatre, and for framing one's life as a quest.

- **Social web**: lodge formats that bind members, create trust, and ease collaboration across professions.

When those three meet a printing press, they shape culture. When they meet a ministry and a secret police, they can shape policy. Wewelsburg shows both the seduction and the catastrophe that follow when myth and bureaucracy interpenetrate. The result was a cult of death with a marble floor and an attendance sheet.

Hidden Orders argues that networks, rituals, and symbols don't just decorate power; they lubricate it. The occult revival shows the mechanism in miniature. A set of ritual tools moved from closed lodges to open culture. An aesthetic became a lifestyle, then a market. And in one corner of Europe, myth took a desk job in a ministry, put on black, and signed off on murder.

The lesson is not that a secret brotherhood runs the world. The lesson is that **symbolic worlds**, when drilled and shared, can be more binding than laws—and more dangerous when they replace them.

Part IV: Shadow Networks of Today

Chapter 10: Bilderberg, Davos, and the New Orders

Let's open the door to the two most misunderstood rooms in the modern architecture of power. One is made of glass—cameras, livestreams, CEOs on panels, prime ministers talking about "resilience," and activists at the mic. That's Davos. The other has frosted windows and a strict guest list. There are no stages, only tables. No press conference. That's Bilderberg. Together they sit at the hinge between the old clubby world of elite conclaves and today's influencer-driven public policy arena. If you want to map how "hidden orders" actually operate in the twenty-first century—how language becomes agenda, how agenda becomes consensus, and how consensus becomes policy—you have to understand both.

What follows is a practical field guide. We'll anchor the history and mechanics of Bilderberg with a clean case study on its origins and secrecy. We'll put Davos alongside it to examine where visibility ends and influence begins. You'll get the analytical tests that help you tell conspiracy theory from open influence, and you'll see the specific channels through which closed-door talk leaks into the bloodstream of the global economy and national politics.

The two rooms: how they work, who shows up, and what "influence" really means

Davos (the World Economic Forum's Annual Meeting) is engineered for optics and broad participation. The 2025 meeting ran 20–24 January under the banner "Collaboration for the Intelligent Age," with public livestreams, open-agenda themes (growth, industries, people, planet, trust), and roughly three thousand participants across governments, business, civil society, academia, and media. In short: a giant mixing chamber whose outputs are narratives, frameworks, and coalitions rather than binding decisions.

Bilderberg is deliberately the opposite. The 71st meeting (12–15 June 2025, Stockholm) invited roughly 120–140 people—heads of government and ministries, central bankers, defense chiefs, chiefs of staff, tech founders, media editors, and strategists—to talk under the Chatham House Rule. The official topics were heavy: the transatlantic relationship, Ukraine, the U.S. economy, Europe, the Middle East, an "authoritarian axis," defense innovation and resilience, AI and national security, proliferation, the geopolitics of energy and critical minerals, and depopulation/migration. There's no communiqué, no vote, no resolutions—just candid debate and the diffusion of ideas among people who can act on them afterward.

The simple contrast that matters

- *Davos: public sessions + livestreams; thousands of attendees; purpose-built for narrative shaping and coalition building across sectors. Output: visible agenda frames and initiatives.*
- *Bilderberg: private discussions; ~120–140 participants; Chatham House Rule; no communiqué. Output: alignment among power centers and shared "situational awareness."*

Two Rooms of Influence

Davos
(World Economic Forum, Annual Meeting)

Public livestreams

Open press briefings

≈ 3,000 participants

≈3,000 participants

Bilderberg
Meeting

🔒 ~120

Meets under the Chatham House Rule

Attendee counts vary by year (WEF ≈3k, Bilderberg ≈120)

Private meetings shaping global policy: the actual mechanics

People imagine back-room deals. What really travels out of these rooms are **frames** (how a problem is defined), **priority lists** (what should be tackled first), and **relationship maps** (who will move first, coordinate, or block). Here's how the machinery usually works:

1. Agenda seeding and vocabulary unification

Before policies exist, there's the language that justifies them. Labels like "economic security," "de-risking," "responsible AI," or "resilience" move from seminar notes to ministerial speeches to G7 communiqués. Closed rooms accelerate a common vocabulary, which then makes intergovernmental work faster because everyone "hears" the same problem.

2. Coalition pre-wiring

A finance minister, a central banker, and three CEOs can turn a hallway conversation into a working channel between their teams. By the time the public sees a "joint statement," informal alignment has already lowered the transaction costs.

3. Red-line testing under the Chatham House Rule

The rule allows participants to probe each other's political red lines without public cost. The **key safeguard** is that no specific speaker can be attributed. This encourages candor but limits accountability. (We'll define the rule precisely below.)

4. Talent scouting and network refresh

Rising figures appear at Davos and, less publicly, at Bilderberg. It's not a magic promotion; it's **exposure** to networks that accelerate careers already on the runway.

5. From frame to policy

The pipeline is usually:

Closed discussion → testable frame → public articulation (speeches, panels) → pilot initiatives → scale via governments/industry/IFIs. Davos emphasizes the public articulation and pilot stage; Bilderberg accelerates the closed-discussion and alignment stage.

The line between conspiracy and open influence

This is where most readers lean forward. How do you tell if a private forum is simply a place to talk—or a place where outsiders are locked out while the insiders decide everyone else's future?

Use these tests:

- **Transparency test**

Does the event publish dates, themes, or attendees? Davos publishes themes and streams sessions; Bilderberg issues a basic topics list and (most years) a participant list—but no sessions or transcripts. The smaller the disclosure, the higher the need for independent scrutiny after the fact.

- **Attribution test (Chatham House Rule)**

The rule says you can use the information but not identify speakers or affiliations. Good for candor; risky because it dilutes accountability. If you want democratic legitimacy, elected officials should report their **policy** positions publicly even if they tested those positions privately.

- **Outcome test**

Are there consistent, specific policy moves that trace back to a given meeting? Causation is rare and hard to prove. More often, you'll see **correlation**: similar policy frames surfacing across capitals after a cycle of private and public convenings.

- **Access test**

Who gets in? Davos is multi-stakeholder; Bilderberg is deliberately narrow. A narrow room can be either efficient or exclusionary. The narrower the room, the stronger the argument for after-action transparency by public officials.

Case Study: The origins and secrecy of the Bilderberg Group

To understand the modern debate, start at the beginning. In the early 1950s, a cosmopolitan Polish political operator—Józef Retinger— worried that anti-American feeling was souring postwar Europe. He convened a private 1952 Paris apartment meeting of senior figures to talk candidly. Two years later, with a royal nudge and organizational help, the concept scaled into a formalized transatlantic meeting at a Dutch country hotel near Arnhem: the Hotel de Bilderberg, whose name the group would keep.

Retinger's "genius move" was to persuade Prince Bernhard of the Netherlands to chair the new forum, instantly conferring status and smoothing invitations to top political and corporate figures across parties and borders. The model worked: a small, confidential environment, no binding outcomes, and a broad ideological mix—by design, conservatives and socialists spoke in the same room when that was unusual. For many years, the "headquarters" was little more than a P.O. Box in Leiden and an answering machine; official posture was icy silence. Over time, the group thawed just enough to issue brief press notices and attendee lists upon request.

The secrecy was not cost-free. In 1976, Prince Bernhard's involvement in the Lockheed bribery scandal forced him to step down and led to the cancellation of that year's meeting—a reminder that even the most discreet networks cannot fully escape public law or public opinion.

What Bilderberg became

By the 1990s and 2000s, "Bilderberg" had entered the culture as a supposed command center of globalization. The reality is simpler and more interesting: it's a **calibration room** for elites already in positions of power. The organization doesn't produce resolutions; it aligns mental models and priorities among people who can implement them later through their governments, companies, or media platforms.

Critics argue that this form of private alignment is precisely the problem—publics feel policy is pre-cooked elsewhere. Defenders counter that sensitive security and economic topics need exactly this space to avoid grandstanding. The truth is that the forum's influence is soft but real: **it shapes consensus, not decrees.**

Modern snapshot (2025)

The 71st meeting in Stockholm listed topics that match the moment: Ukraine; the transatlantic relationship; AI as a national-security variable; defense innovation; energy and critical minerals; migration and depopulation. The format remained unchanged: Chatham House Rule, no votes, no resolutions. The participant list mixed elected leaders, central bankers, tech founders, editors, CEOs, NATO, and EU officials. That's the pattern—small, cross-functional, high-decision-authority.

Davos as the "open" counterpart—what it does (and doesn't) do

Davos wears its process on its sleeve: themes published in advance; livestreamed sessions; a press corps; civil society and academic participation; and community tracks like Young Global Leaders and

---

Bilderberg timeline (useful waypoints)
- *1952: First exploratory Paris meeting (private apartment).*
- *1954: Formal launch at Hotel de Bilderberg, Oosterbeek. Name sticks.*
- *1976: Lockheed scandal; Prince Bernhard resigns; meeting cancelled.*
- *2000s–2010s: Modest increase in public information (press notes, partial lists).*
- *2024: Meeting in Madrid (published topics and list).*
- *2025: Meeting in Stockholm; topics dominated by security, AI, energy, and migration.*

Global Shapers. In 2025, the umbrella theme was "Collaboration for the Intelligent Age," grouping sessions under reimagining growth, industries in transition, investing in people, safeguarding the planet, and rebuilding trust. The value proposition is clear: **visibility + convening power = faster coalition building**.

But transparency has limits. The public stage is only part of Davos; private breakfasts, bilateral meetings, and off-record dinners are where many deals and pledges get shaped. And while the Forum publishes attendance and streams sessions, participation requires membership or invitation. Networking density is the point—and that looks exclusionary to critics, especially when global inequities are the topic.

The overlap and the friction: where Davos and Bilderberg meet

- Person-level overlap

Some individuals shuttle between the two: ministers, central bankers, international organization chiefs, Fortune 100 CEOs, and

How to read Davos outputs intelligently

- *Don't overvalue big panel quotes. Watch the follow-through: new steering groups, public-private initiatives, or corporate/sovereign pledges launched in Q1–Q3.*
- *Track cross-panel repeaters (phrases and priorities echoed by central bankers, CEOs, and ministers). That's your frame migration.*
- *Check whether a Davos pledge gets budgeted (public money) or integrated (corporate KPIs). If not, it was theater.*

the editors or columnists who craft how the rest of us will read the world next week. Those networks are the "shadow wiring" behind policy coordination.

- **Topic-level overlap**

Security, technology, energy, and the macroeconomy are now fused. You saw this in Stockholm's agenda (AI + deterrence; defense innovation; energy critical minerals) and in Davos's "Intelligent Age" framing (AI across industries and governance). The same problem set, two different operating systems.

- **Norm friction**

Davos leans on legitimacy via openness and multi-stakeholder breadth. Bilderberg's legitimacy claim is competence and candor: a small, trusted group can be brutally realistic. In democracies, **both** can be valid—**provided** officials answer publicly for what they support privately.

Responsible scrutiny: how to investigate without lapsing into myth

If you're writing, researching, or just trying to be an informed citizen, here's the practical approach:

1. **Anchor facts where the organizations publish them**

For Bilderberg: use the annual press release (dates, city, topics) and the posted participant list; they're sparse but official. For Davos: the event site, themes, and the public sessions index are abundant.

2. **Map the post-meeting signal.**

Collect speeches, budget drafts, regulatory notices, and corporate filings in the 90–180 days after the events. Look for the same phrases and priorities reappearing. That's how frames travel.

3. **Disaggregate "influence"**

Separate **agenda-setting** (what leaders talk about) from **policy-making** (what they enact). A televised panel can change nothing; a 15-minute private meeting can trigger a change order. But you need evidence, not vibes.

4. Demand after-action transparency from public officials

Chatham House Rule guards candor; it does not absolve democratic accountability. Public office holders should state their positions and intended votes clearly back home—even if they refined those positions in private.

A closer lens: Bilderberg's built-in secrecy, explained plainly

- **Why the P.O. Box aura?**

Historically, the group maintained the thinnest possible public footprint—no headquarters tour, no media day. That minimized political noise and protected attendee candor. Only in recent decades has it issued press notes and posted attendees.

- **Who picks the guest list?**

A small steering committee (two representatives from ~18 countries, rotating over time) shapes invitations to maintain geographic and functional balance (politics, finance, defense, media, academia). The list changes yearly; it's not a membership club.

- **Does it swing elections or pick presidents?**

That's the claim you'll hear. The more defensible reading is **"elite due diligence"**: the room exposes rising politicians to peers and donors; those politicians already have momentum. Exposure accelerates trajectories, but it's not a magic scepter.

- **Where does it go wrong?**

When private consensus drifts into **policy lock-in** without public debate. That risk is highest in security and tech (AI, cyber, surveillance), where timelines are fast and public understanding lags. The counterweight is parliamentary oversight, strong press follow-up, and civil society expertise in the room when policies become public.

Semiconductors Climate Quantum
Ukraine NATO Cybersecurity Inrtio
Supply Chains Inflation Inflation
Hydro- **AI** Green Transition Elections TTC
gen **Defense**
Nuclear
Nuclear Green Transition Indo-Paccifriic
Energy Middle East Space
Industrial Policy LNG
Green Transition
Hydrogen **Transatlantic**
Nuclear **Migration** Migration
Offshore Wind Policy
LNG Sanctions Migrationn Policy Migration Policy
China Migration Policy Asylum Rare Earths EV
Batteries ESG
Indecmn Demographics Remittances Resilience

Davos's value—beyond the panels

Three real values keep Davos relevant:

- **Cross-sector docking**

Government meets capital meets science meets civil society in one place. That doesn't guarantee wisdom, but it shortens the path from idea to prototype.

- **Narrative reframing at scale**

When the Forum declares a theme like "Collaboration for the Intelligent Age," it packages dozens of working sessions under a coherent arc. That helps busy decision-makers make sense of complexity and align their own internal messaging.

- **Legitimacy through visibility**

The livestreams, the public agenda, the Open Forum—these don't eliminate power asymmetries, but they raise the **cost** of bad arguments. When a minister or CEO says something on stage, it's on the record and easy to challenge later.

When influence turns into pressure: ethical lines to watch

- **From convening to gatekeeping**

When a small circle repeatedly defines the "reasonable" range of debate, out-of-consensus views get starved of oxygen. Remedy: wider expert participation when the issue moves from framing to rule-making.

- **From expertise to capture**

On tech policy (AI, platforms, cyber), the experts often work at the firms being regulated. Remedy: conflict-of-interest hygiene— disclose roles; diversify expert panels; invite public-interest technologists.

- **From cross-border alignment to domestic blind spots**

Policymakers can "overlearn" elite international consensus and underweight domestic median voters. Remedy: elected officials must translate private alignment into public arguments at home—and win them.

Why the myths persist—and what to do with them

Secrecy plus status equals mythology. Bilderberg's frosted glass guarantees suspicion. Davos's stages guarantee backlash. Yet the serious investigator avoids two traps: (1) the comforting belief that nothing important happens in private; (2) the equally comforting belief that everything important does.

The balanced posture is simple: **assume influence, demand evidence.** Learn how frames move. Check who was in the room. Then test whether those frames show up in budgets, rulebooks, and market moves.

Chapter 11

The Vatican and the Black Nobility

You're about to walk into a room most people only glimpse from the outside. Some of what follows has been mythologized for centuries; some of it is documented and humdrum; some of it is genuinely startling once you put the pieces together. Our job in this chapter is to separate signal from noise—while keeping our curiosity cranked up to eleven.

We'll move with a clear plan:

1. Map the **real** secret orders and para-orders clustered around the Catholic Church;

2. Probe the **claims** about hidden archives and covert channels of influence and measure them against what's actually known;

3. Dig into a concrete **case study**—the Society of Jesus (Jesuits)—to see how global reach, internal discipline, and tactical flexibility turn a small elite into a world-spanning network.

Along the way, you'll see why the same handful of corridors, chapels, villas, and hilltop compounds keep showing up in serious histories *and* in late-night whisper networks—often for very different reasons.

The Claim of a "Black Nobility," and What It Actually Refers To

The phrase **"Black Nobility"** is a slippery one. In the broadest conspiratorial usage, it's said to mean a web of old aristocratic families—Roman and Italian above all—who maintained their power by aligning with the papacy when it ruled central Italy, then updated their methods for the modern state, financial capitalism, and media age. The press releases for this idea usually toss in surnames like

Colonna, Orsini, Borghese, Chigi, Medici, and others; they'll imply dynastic ties to bankers, diplomats, and—inevitably—secret societies. The darker spin says these families formed a standing committee behind Popes, cardinals, and Vatican diplomats; the lighter, more historical take is simply that aristocratic clans do what aristocratic clans have always done—marry, lobby, fund, endow, and, when cornered, make deals.

Here's the sober baseline:

- For centuries, **noble patronage** and **curial politics** were intertwined. That's not a secret; it's how Europe worked.

- The papal court and the Roman patriciate had mutual dependencies—land, offices, military protection, and marriages.

- In the 19th–20th centuries, strong nation-states and modern law eroded hereditary leverage, but **vestigial influence** persisted through charities, Vatican-linked orders, and social capital.

So is there a permanent, hidden "board of directors"? Evidence for a formalized, perpetual shadow cabinet is weak. Evidence for **durable networks**—families, orders, financiers, and foundations who know how to get a papal meeting or move a shipment through customs—is strong. The difference matters, and we'll keep it in view.

Secret Orders Within the Catholic World: What's Real, What's Rumor

When people say "secret orders" of the Church, three names dominate the modern imagination: **the Jesuits, Opus Dei, and the Sovereign Military Order of Malta**. Only one of those is a religious order in the strict sense (the Jesuits). The others are distinct canonical or sovereign entities with their own legal nuances.

The Society of Jesus (Jesuits)

Founded in 1540, the Jesuits are a religious order under vows, with global missions in education, research, spiritual direction, and diplomacy. Their reputation for stealth and strategy comes from real traits: rigorous formation, a mobile deployment model, and a tradition of advising rulers and educating elites. We'll unpack their global method in the case study below.

A telling European episode, though, hints at their **operational culture** under pressure: in Elizabethan and Jacobean England, lay collaborators engineered **"priest holes"**—hidden chambers—to conceal Jesuit missionaries from searches that could last days, complete with decoy carpentry, feeding tubes embedded within mortar, and grueling, clandestine labor by a master artisan, **Nicholas Owen** (who died under torture and was later canonized). This was **tradecraft** in a religious war, not myth.

Opus Dei (The Prelature of the Holy Cross and Opus Dei)

Opus Dei is a **personal prelature**—a modern canonical structure—whose lay members are encouraged to pursue sanctity through everyday work and family life, with a minority living celibately in dedicated centers. Outsiders often project thriller-novel fantasies onto the group, but the world headquarters at **Villa Tevere** in Rome feels more like a discreet professional service firm than a torch-lit crypt. The membership is largely lay, the priests are a tiny fraction, and the internal culture emphasizes discipline over drama. Even the oft-discussed penitential practices are limited and regulated; sensational tropes don't hold up against the mundane reality described by careful observers.

VILLA TEVERE
VIALE BRUNO BUOZZI

Meeting

Chapel

Crypt

The Sovereign Military Order of Malta (SMOM)

The **Knights of Malta** are part relic, part powerhouse: an ancient chivalric/religious order that today also operates as a **sovereign entity** with diplomatic relations, humanitarian logistics, and a global medical footprint. In Rome, their **Magistral Palace** on **Via dei Condotti** is extraterritorial; their **Aventine** compound—**the Magistral Villa (Villa Malta)**—is famed for that "keyhole" view lining up the dome of St. Peter's. Their special status means their cars carry distinctive plates; they've even operated a **Magistral Post Office** issuing their own stamps with bilateral postal arrangements. It looks quaint. In practice, it's a soft-power dream: hospitaller missions move **fast** thanks to status, protocol, and relationships.

Hidden Corridors, Locked Chapels, and the "Secret Archive" Idea

Secrecy has a physical geography in Rome. Three sites make the idea of "hidden Vatican worlds" feel tangible, and that tangibility is why they're so often over-read in conspiracy lore.

The Passetto di Borgo: Escape Route in Stone

The **Passetto** is an enclosed passageway—part of the Leonine Wall—linking the Vatican to **Castel Sant'Angelo**. Built and improved across centuries (notably by **Nicholas III** and **Alexander VI**), it allowed popes to flee in emergencies. During the 1527 Sack of Rome, **Clement VII** used it to reach safety while the Swiss Guard fought a doomed rear-guard action. The details—hidden windows that look like loopholes, the way the wall feigns a defensive crown while masking a passage—explain why the Passetto becomes a cinematic stand-in for Vatican secrecy. It's less a symbol of occult power than of **contingency planning** in a dangerous city.

Sancta Sanctorum and the Pauline Chapel: Privacy at the Core

Inside the old **Lateran Palace** sits the **Sancta Sanctorum**—a very private papal oratory with relics, ancient art, and a reputation for gravity. Access is highly restricted; Mass is reserved for the Pope. This is not a Dan-Brown set; it's simply how sacred spaces of the medieval papal household functioned—tight control, curated visibility, heavy symbolism.

A short walk away, inside the Apostolic Palace, the **Pauline Chapel** (Cappella Paolina) is where cardinals gather at the very start of a conclave before moving to the Sistine Chapel. It houses late Michelangelo frescoes—**Conversion of Saul** and **Crucifixion of Peter**—and is generally closed to the public. Over the decades, it has also been a magnet for **apocalyptic anecdotes**. The most sensational—

of a black-mass-like "enthronement of Lucifer" in the early 1960s—circulates due to a novelist and ex-Jesuit who insisted (with guarded wording) that his fiction mirrored fact. Whether you find that credible or not, the **chapel's privacy** is the real accelerant here: what cannot be seen becomes easy to mythologize.

"Secret Archives" vs. The Vatican Archives

Much of the mystique gathers around the term **Archivum Secretum Vaticanum**—"secret" only in the archaic sense of "private" or "for the sovereign's personal use." The modern archive (renamed the Vatican Apostolic Archive) is controlled, but scholars do receive access by application; catalogs and critical editions keep expanding. Are there locked funds that will never be opened? Of course, every sovereign archive in the world has classified material. But the idea of a singular, world-breaking vault that would rewrite human history if opened tomorrow is a **narrative device**, not a demonstrated fact.

We've just looked at **real** locked spaces (Sancta Sanctorum, Pauline Chapel) and a **real** escape route (Passetto). Those prove private zones exist. They don't prove omnipotent cover-ups. The burden of proof stays with anyone making epoch-shaking claims.

Where Finance Meets Piety: Orders, Banks, and the "Shadow" Label

One reason the "Black Nobility" label sticks is that elite Catholic ecosystems **interface cleanly with private banking** and discreet wealth management. That doesn't make them nefarious; it makes them old, organized, and comfortable with protocol.

Take the **Knights of Malta** again. Their sovereign status, diplomatic ties, posts, and plates look ceremonial; they also grease wheels for humanitarian shipments and medical services across dozens of countries. You can stand at their gate on Via dei Condotti and watch that blend of **pageantry and logistics** in action. It's not "shadow rule." It's institutional memory applied to service, with benefits that sometimes feel like **cheat codes** in a bureaucratic world.

Zoom out and you'll find that private finance has its own mystique— Swiss banquiers privés, City of London houses, and durable family firms. Their longevity and discretion mean they often surface in the same chapters as old orders, whether you're reading about **Rothschild** at New Court, **Lazard**'s clubby advisory culture, or the very "private" courtyards of **Coutts** at 440 Strand. The overlap between **elite Catholic patrons, aristocratic families**, and **bankers** is historical sociology before it's a conspiracy. It's what happens when influence migrates across salons, embassies, and clinics.

How to Read "Shadow" Claims]

Step 1: Map the legal status (order, prelature, sovereign entity, NGO).
Step 2: Track the logistics (diplomatic pouches, extraterritorial sites, customs privileges).
Step 3: Follow the funding (endowments, donors, bankers).
Step 4: Cross-check for public outputs (hospitals, schools, relief convoys).
Step 5: Demand documents, not vibes.

Case Study: The Jesuits and Their Global Reach

If you want to see a "hidden order" actually functioning as a **global operating system**, study the **Society of Jesus**. A few core ideas explain why they show up everywhere, from world-class universities to refugee camps to quiet rooms where a head of state wants spiritual counsel.

1) Mission as Mobility

From their founding, Jesuits were structured for **deployment**. They could be in Goa, Beijing, or Quebec within a single generation of the order's birth, learning languages, studying local cultures, and building institutions that would outlive them.

When states turned hostile, they adapted. In England, that meant covert ministry and the kind of **counter-surveillance architecture** we saw above. In other theaters, it meant the opposite—high visibility: colleges, printing presses, catechisms in local tongues. The same corporate DNA produced **underground** patience and **public** excellence.

2) Education as Power

By investing in **schools and universities**, Jesuits placed their ideas where elites are formed. That's not sinister; it's strategic. Educate the lawyers, scientists, and ministers of tomorrow, and you raise the quality of civic life while seeding the culture with your worldview. The method is scalable and sticky: alumni networks persist, and those networks—not secret handshakes—are what people often misread as "shadow control."

3) Spiritual Tools for Decision-Makers

The **Spiritual Exercises** teach discernment under pressure. If you've ever watched a CEO or a cabinet minister walk through structured reflection, you know it's rare in secular institutions. Jesuits export that structure. You don't need to buy the theology to see the tactical value:

clearer choices, deeper conscience checks, and better emotional calibration under stress.

4) The "Intel" Reputation—Explained

Why the aura of spymastery? Partly because of history—Jesuits were **advisers** to kings, confessors to queens, astronomers to emperors. Partly because their vow-based discipline looks like clandestine training to outsiders. And partly because in some eras they really did operate **behind enemy lines**, using cover, codes, and safe houses as tools of survival. Elizabethan priest-hunters earned their own grim reputation because Jesuit tradecraft forced them to step up their countermeasures. The **Nicholas Owen** story is enough to explain why the Society's name still makes certain governments twitch.

Jesuit Tradecraft (Elizabethan England)
- *Hides within hides: multiple decoys to outlast multi-day searches.*
- *Feeding tubes in mortar to sustain trapped clergy.*
- *Night work by a single artisan to reduce leaks; public "day jobs" to mask intent.*

Where Legends Accrete: From Borgias to Prophecy

If you walk the Vatican at night, you can almost hear the older stories: cardinals jockeying, embassies buzzing, rumors rippling down marble halls. This is fertile soil; legends grow quickly. A few recurring motifs:

- **Renaissance decadence** (cue the Borgias) gets used as a template for every era—usually lazily. Some courtiers were indeed corrupt; others were reformers. The archive of behavior is mixed, not uniformly monstrous.

- **Prophecy lists** (e.g., attributions to **St. Malachy**) spike in popularity during turmoil. Even sophisticated readers can be seduced by an ominous Latin tag that seems to fit a 20th-century Pope. It's compelling; it's also contested and likely a much later construction. Read them as cultural artifacts first, predictions second.

- **Black rites in private chapels?** As we saw with the **Pauline Chapel**, **privacy + anxiety** can equal unforgettable urban legends. Source them to named witnesses and documents or treat them as what they are: stories.

The Black Nobility Today: Influence Without a Crown

How to Test a Vatican Story

1. Name the witnesses (titles, dates, locations).
2. Check the space (is it publicly accessible? who controls access?).
3. Look for corroboration (independent diaries, letters, police reports).
4. Ask what the physical plant allows (antiquated locks? guards? CCTV?).
5. When you hit a wall: file it under legend, not fact.

Does a Roman noble name still open doors? In certain situations, yes—especially in **cultural diplomacy**, **heritage conservation**, and **elite Catholic philanthropy**. Does an aristocratic surname automatically equal control over Popes or orders? No. The modern Church is a multinational, multi-lingual body with electoral rules, transparency pressures, and constant media scrutiny. What endures is **social gravity**: old families, old orders, and old banks keep orbiting one another because they share habits of discretion, protocol literacy, and a reflex for **getting things done quietly**.

One place where this can look like "shadow" mastery is **logistics**—pushing medical cargo through a balky port thanks to a phone call from a knight-ambassador; routing a high-stakes meeting through a villa with extraterritorial status; slipping relief cash into a conflict zone via an old family's humanitarian foundation. That's not smokey backrooms; it's **institutional memory**, and it's often beneficial on the ground.

Humanitarian Donation Flow:
Private Bank → Order's Rome HQ → Field Hosp

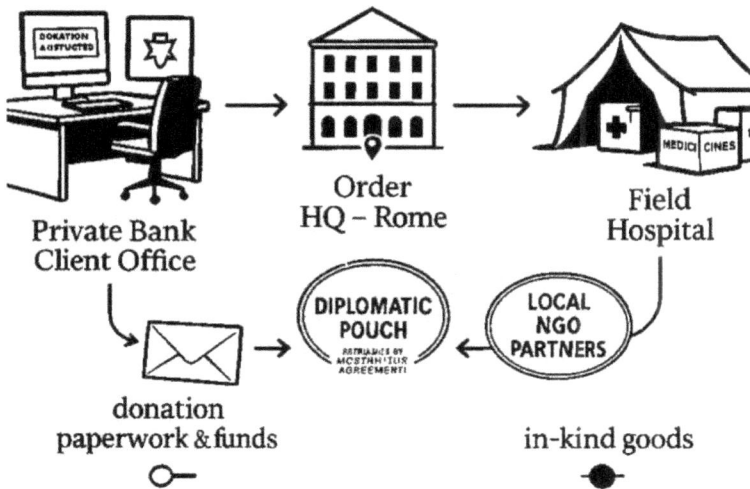

Private Bank
Client Office

Order
HQ – Rome

Field
Hospital

DIPLOMATIC
POUCH

LOCAL
NGO
PARTNERS

donation
paperwork & funds

in-kind goods

Sober Bottom Line on "Covert Influence"

1. **Orders are not interchangeable.** A Jesuit province, a personal prelature, and a sovereign chivalric order have different charters, oversight, and accountabilities. Put them in one basket and you'll misread everything.

2. **Privacy isn't proof of malice.** Closed chapels, private archives, gated compounds—these are normal in religious capitals and old cities. Treat access control as a **variable to analyze**, not a verdict.

3. **Networks beat hierarchies** in Rome. If you're searching for one master switch, you'll be disappointed. The city runs on relationships, favors, and remembered debts—subtle, often non-linear, and resistant to flowcharts.

4. **The Black Nobility idea has *diagnostic* value** if you use it to track historic families and their foundations across time. It turns toxic when you reify it into a monolith that explains everything.

The Jesuits, Revisited: Tactics You Can Actually See

To make this as concrete as possible, let's throw a spotlight on **five Jesuit "habits"** that translate into global reach:

(A) Embed locally. Learn the language; respect the culture; build schools that outlast politics. That's why Jesuit institutions worldwide feel simultaneously European, Asian, African, and American.

(B) Play the long game. Suppression, exile, restoration—Jesuit history is a sine wave, and the Society is designed to survive it. Archives, alumni, and intellectual capital cushion the dips.

(C) Use small teams. A handful of disciplined operators gets more done than a bloated bureaucracy. In hostile climates, that means stealth; in friendly ones, it means **excellence on display.**

(D) Influenced by formation, not fiat. Educate decision-makers; accompany them in conscience; leave the visible levers to politicians.

(E) Keep your tech updated. From early printing to observatories and today's data-driven social ministries, Jesuit works tend to sit at the edge where faith meets tools.

A single Elizabethan example—**the priest holes built by Nicholas Owen**—illustrates (A) through (C): local knowledge, long-term patience, tiny teams, and tradecraft appropriate to the threat.

Final Synthesis: Hidden Orders, Open Outputs

When you hear "hidden orders" and "shadow networks," you're really hearing about **plausible deniability** married to **institutional competence.** People who can get things done in quiet, technically fussy systems (customs, visas, permits, licensing, port clearance, bishop's conference schedules) will always look like magicians from the outside. The Vatican world—orders, prelatures, patricians, and private bankers—has a lot of those people.

If you want the practical truth and not the bedtime story, look for **outputs** and **jurisdictions:**

- Outputs: hospitals opened, clinics stocked, students graduated, archives cataloged.

- Jurisdictions: extraterritorial gates, diplomatic plates, canonical charters—these are **levers** anyone can study without believing in a super-conspiracy.

That's the grown-up way to read the Vatican and the so-called Black Nobility. And it turns out to be a lot more interesting than a single villain in a velvet mask.

Chapter 12

Hidden Orders in the Digital Age

You're holding a flashlight in a power outage. The old landmarks—lodges, clubhouses, back rooms—are dim silhouettes. But in the beam, new structures jump out: clouds you can't touch, feeds you can't see, private listservs and encrypted channels where reputations, funding, and policies move at speed. That's the core shift of this chapter: the center of gravity has moved from the visible stage to the invisible network. The names still sound familiar—board chairs, think tanks, elite conferences—but the wiring behind them is different. Today, code, capital, and closed channels do what stone buildings, oath-bound fraternities, and discreet salons once did.

From lodges and bunkers to clouds and backchannels

It helps to start with the "visible secret" of the past. In the twentieth century, secrecy often had an address: a Vauxhall Cross stronghold for an intelligence service, a sovereign listening post in Yorkshire, or a mountain complex designed to keep government running under threat. These were purpose-built nerve centers where gatekeeping was literal—doors, fences, moats, and access lists. The modern era didn't end that infrastructure, but it changed the primary vector of influence. Today, most elite coordination doesn't need a fortress; it needs a channel. The room is a Signal thread; the policy draft is a collaborative doc; the pressure campaign is a "friends of friends" chat spun up after an invite-only summit.

When we point to a hotel that gave a famous private group its name—or to a university "tomb" where future power brokers rehearsed bonding rituals—we're really tracking an older operating system of secrecy. Those physical anchors mattered (and still do), but in a networked age, the most consequential contents are not in a vault;

they're in an ever-moving flow of messages, commits, and capital calls. The modern "hidden order" is not a room—it's a route.

For context on how earlier "secrecy with an address" worked—from underground continuity-of-government sites to infamous test ranges and elite collegiate societies—see the documented accounts of Mount Weather and Area 51, and the long tradition of Yale's senior societies shaping cohorts.

How power has shifted into invisible networks

Old vs. New Hidden Orders

Old: fixed sites, ritual membership, slow cycles, secrecy through walls.
New: mobile platforms, fluid membership, fast cycles, secrecy through encryption and informal norm.

The network advantage

Networks beat institutions when speed, reach, and plausible deniability matter. A closed Slack of fund managers coordinating a rescue round; a backchannel of policy entrepreneurs aligning talking points before a hearing; a private research list harmonizing risk narratives across AI labs. None of that requires a charter. It requires trust, timing, and a curator.

Three reasons networks dominate:

1. **Latency:** You can align a dozen decision-makers in an hour with a single thread.

2. **Surface area:** You can attach to media, regulators, or standards groups quickly through overlapping members.

3. **Shadow optionality:** If a narrative backfires, the network disbands itself; the institution can't.

The stack of digital-era influence

Think of an influence "stack" with four layers:

- **Compute & Code:** Whoever controls scarce compute, core model weights, or widely adopted protocols shapes the feasible set.

- **Capital & Coverage:** Venture funds and strategic investors convert that feasibility into dominance; insurance and legal coverage de-risk it.

- **Community & Credentialing:** Invite-only fellowships, semi-public forums, and private campuses create a shared language and an informal vetting pipeline.

- **Convenings & Choreography:** Annual, off-the-record gatherings set alignment for the year: who's "in the room," which themes get airtime, and which deals look inevitable.

Corporate elites, think tanks, and the modern choreography of secrecy

A generation ago, the shorthand for "shadow influence" was a handful of elite clubs and annual conclaves. Many still operate. The point isn't to mystify them, but to understand their function in a networked field.

- **Secretive deal camps:** The Allen & Co. Sun Valley conference has long served as a "summer camp for billionaires," a tightly managed environment where media and tech chiefs mingle, test narratives, and sometimes pave the way for major transactions. Recent cycles show AI and defense-tech at the top of the agenda.

- **Invite-only geopolitical salons:** Bilderberg continues to convene senior figures from business, tech, and politics under Chatham House rules; the 2025 meeting in Stockholm published its participant list while keeping discussions private. The point is not occult ritual; it's controlled context and curated access.

- **Policy keystones with corporate on-ramps:** The Council on Foreign Relations runs a Corporate Program that explicitly links private-sector leaders to policy makers and CFR experts via briefings and events; the roster includes major tech and finance firms, formalizing a professional backchannel between corporate and state actors.

- **Transregional strategy networks:** The Trilateral Commission's regional meetings—for example, in Silicon Valley in late 2024—frame technology risk and opportunity discussions for a cross-sector mix of leaders under non-attribution rules.

- **Meta-think tank networks:** The Atlas Network openly positions itself as a "think tank that builds think tanks," providing training and coordination to hundreds of partners worldwide. Regardless of one's politics, that's an infrastructure for idea distribution and agenda-setting.

The choreography has evolved, but the effect is familiar: information advantages, narrative harmonization, and faster coalition formation than the public, formal sphere typically permits.

Earlier eras also blended secrecy and access: discrete steering committees and invite lists around the famous hotel that lent its name to a private transatlantic forum; private banks and clubs that screened participants long before any formal title. The line from those rooms to today's encrypted channels is continuity, not rupture.

Tech "cults of secrecy": subcultures, manifestos, and moral math

"Cult" is a loaded term. Here we use it in the analytical sense: tightly bonded communities with shared esoteric language, initiation pathways, and high commitment norms. Digital-era versions often publish manifestos and hold public meetups—yet operate gated backchannels where the real alignment happens.

Techno-optimism and e/acc

The "techno-optimist" current argues that society's duty is to accelerate technological growth, with minimal constraint. Venture figures have articulated this in sweeping essays, now widely circulated in boardrooms and congressional hearing prep. A related memeplex, "effective accelerationism" (e/acc), pushes this ethos to the edge: progress first, regulate later, if at all. Supporters frame it as civilizational vitality; critics warn it dismisses safety and externalities.

Rationalists, long-termists, and the moral calculus of the far future

The rationalist and effective-altruist ecosystems built reputational engines around reason, cause prioritization, and, in some corners, safeguarding the far future (longtermism). These scenes incubated training camps, fellowships, and donor circles, and they significantly influenced how AI risk is framed today. The movement is diverse; its critics argue that rarefied moral math can rationalize reckless trade-offs, while supporters say it injects rigor where vibes used to suffice. Public reporting has scrutinized both the positive and the troubling edges of these communities.

Moral Philosophy:
Idea → Institution → Influence

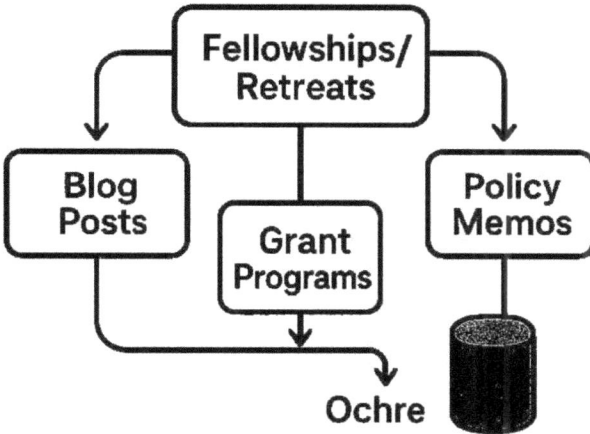

When subculture meets scandal

The FTX collapse didn't just wreck a crypto exchange; it splashed moral hazard onto philanthropic networks linked to effective altruism, forcing reconsideration of governance and due diligence when ideology and money entwine. The conversation since has been: how to keep the epistemic rigor while designing guardrails that resist reputational laundering.

In parallel, the Bay Area has seen fringe offshoots around AI apocalypse narratives and identity-loaded subcultures; journalists have documented the damage when charismatic leaders exploit high-commitment norms. These are cautionary tales about how "secrecy" and "specialness" can become cover for abuse—a risk in any tight-bond scene.

The security-state feedback loop: startups, venture, and intelligence

The cleanest throughline from twentieth-century "secret state" to twenty-first-century "secret network" is the capital-tech-intel triangle. The CIA's strategic investor, In-Q-Tel, backed tools that became core to government analytics; that imprimatur conferred credibility in commercial markets and helped define a genre—defense-tech startups oriented to public-sector demand. Today, a new wave of investors is explicitly building in this space, with rising budgets and geopolitical friction as tailwinds.

If past "big ears" and secret campuses handled interception and continuity, the new layer is model-mediated intelligence and battlefield autonomy—again, with the sensitive parts living behind NDAs and access-controlled repos as much as behind fences.

Case Study: Silicon Valley and the rise of new esoteric ideologies

The Valley is a convening circuit with a creed

Silicon Valley is not just a place; it's a circuit: accelerators and fellowships that act like secular seminaries, annual billionaire camps in Idaho where the year's master story is rehearsed, and boutique fellowships that skip the usual credentials to elevate the "exceptional." The selection and bonding functions once handled by collegiate societies or gentlemen's clubs now run through demo days, founder houses, private campuses, and syndicate chats.

- **Sun Valley's function:** It's a narrative and deal thermostat. If AI and defense are hot at Sun Valley, the rest of the calendar takes note.

- **Fellowships as a pipeline:** Programs like the Thiel Fellowship explicitly re-route talent away from traditional gatekeepers into an alternative patronage system with dense alumni ties.

- **Mafias that aren't criminal:** "X-Mafia" labels (PayPal being the archetype) describe alumni webs that cross-backed companies, staffed boards, and seeded new funds. The point isn't illegality; it's cohesion and path-dependent advantage.

Ideologies with operating instructions

Several Valley-adjacent ideologies are not just beliefs; they're roadmaps:

- **Techno-optimism / e/acc:** "Push the throttle." The operational advice is to seek energy abundance, scale AI fast, and treat regulatory constraints as value-destroying drag.

- **Longtermism:** "Maximize expected value across centuries." That can justify focusing on AI alignment or biosecurity; critics say it can also excuse near-term harms.

- **Network states:** "Assemble a cloud community first, then negotiate territory and recognition later." It's a programmatic approach to sovereignty via networks.

Each provides a moral warrant for action and a recruitment filter. Each travels through the stack: manifesto → community → capital → policy conversation.

Governance drama as x-ray: the OpenAI episode

When a frontier AI lab went through a boardroom crisis, the world got a glimpse of how overlapping networks—employees, investors, partners, and public officials—apply pressure in real time. The speed of coalition-forming, the use of open letters, and the platform leverage of strategic partners were textbook network moves. Regardless of who you root for, the episode demonstrated how "hidden orders" operate in the open-ish: publicly visible moves coordinated by private backchannels.

Defense-tech revival and the return of raison d'état

With geopolitical shocks and a deteriorating security environment, investment and policymaking tilted toward dual-use platforms. You could watch the narrative tighten: "move fast" migrated from phones to drones, from clicks to kilowatts. A new cohort of VCs positioned defense as a moral imperative, not just a market. That shift is measurable in funding, company formation, and procurement reforms.

The data-broker shadow market

Much of Silicon Valley's influence rides on data advantages. Around the Valley—but also far beyond it—data brokers build dossiers and sell access. Regulators have begun to push back, citing harms around sensitive location tracking, discrimination, and unaccountable surveillance economics. This isn't cloak-and-dagger; it's terms-and-conditions and third-party SDKs. The "hidden order" is a spreadsheet.

Corporate elites, think tanks, and tech cults—how the pieces fit

Here's the joint:

- **Think tanks** translate network narratives into policy furniture—reports, Hill briefings, respectable panels—while offering the corporate program "door" that makes sensitive conversations ordinary.

- **Elite convenings** synchronize messaging and set deal velocity for the quarter or year, with under-the-radar side meetings that do the real work.

- **Tech subcultures** supply the visionary language, the fellowship pipelines, and the rhetorical energy that attracts talent and capital.

- **Strategic capital** (including state-adjacent capital) scales the winners and embeds them in national strategies.

None of this requires conspiracy in the cinematic sense. It's choreography—structured serendipity—by a relatively small set of curators who know each other.

Practical fieldcraft for readers: mapping hidden orders ethically

1. **Start with calendars and credits.** Track recurring events, advisory boards, and acknowledgments in white papers. Who appears across several?

2. **Map the curators.** Look for the people who convene, not just those who keynote.

3. **Trace capital pathways.** Early strategic checks often predict policy footprints later.

4. **Decode the lexicon.** Every network has a codebook. Learn the phrases that unlock rooms.

5. **Separate signal from myth.** Many elite gatherings publish lists and themes. Focus on who follows up with concrete coalitions or budget lines.

Balanced reading of "secrecy" today

What secrecy still does well: It lowers rhetorical heat so rivals can cooperate; it lets founders and officials share hard numbers; it creates a zone for "pilot" consensus before the cameras roll.

Where secrecy fails: It breeds hubris, groupthink, and blind spots; it can launder reputations; it can tilt the field against outsiders who lack the right introductions.

The aim isn't to romanticize hidden orders or to demonize them. It's to render them visible enough for accountability without destroying the legitimate need for private coordination in complex systems.

The older world of private steering groups and senior societies shows the allure and the risk: the ability to form tight bonds and force big questions in a small room, and the danger of mistaking exclusivity for wisdom. Today's networks are faster and larger—but the human failure modes are the same.

Seeing the wires

If you're looking for the modern "tomb" or "lodge," you'll miss it. The room is the route; the vault is the version-controlled repo; the oath is an NDA and a calendar invite. The best defense against unhealthy shadow power is not paranoia; it's pattern recognition, public-interest OSINT, and institutions that can absorb new information without panic.

Part V: The Patterns and the Future

Chapter 13: The Language of Symbols

Open the dossier, pull up a chair, and run a finger over the ink that never dries. The most powerful messages in the history of hidden orders were not whispered—they were carved in stone, painted into ceilings, stitched into robes, choreographed into processions, and diffused into coins, seals, and flags. Words can be censored, burned, or mistranslated. Symbols slip past censors because they appear to be decoration, habit, or heritage. This chapter decodes how and why secret fraternities and shadow networks have relied on visual and spatial language; why identical motifs surface centuries apart and continents away; and how one emblem—the all-seeing eye—has traveled from temples to government seals to today's memes without losing its uncanny charge.

Why hidden orders speak in architecture, art, and ritual

The first rule of quiet power is deniability. A building with a particular façade can always be "just a building." A pattern on the floor can be "just a design." But to an initiate trained to read it, that façade becomes a sentence, and that pattern becomes an instruction.

Symbols outperform words for eight hardheaded reasons:

1. **Durability.** Stone and bronze outlive archives and regimes. A ritual outlives its founders because it's stored in bodies and habits.

2. **Ambiguity on demand.** The same emblem can carry one meaning for the public and a deeper layer for insiders.

3. **Memory efficiency.** Ritual sequences (east to west, dark to light, three to five to seven) encode doctrine as a route you can walk.

4. **Recruitment and filtering.** Costly, elaborate symbols and rituals screen for commitment—the more time and resources demanded, the fewer dilettantes make it through.

5. **Camouflage in plain sight.** Common architectural features (domes, pillars, grids) provide cover for "overwrites"—subtle tweaks that telegraph membership, hierarchy, or allegiance.

6. **Jurisdictional safety.** In eras when speech was dangerous, a carved frieze could preach what a pamphlet could not.

7. **Transmission without paper.** Initiates can reproduce a symbol's proportions with a compass and straightedge from memory.

8. **Emotional priming.** Architecture manipulates light, height, echo, and threshold to get the body to feel the doctrine before the mind explains it.

Why Architecture Beats Pamphlets
- *Stone lasts longer than laws.*
- *Ambiguity is a feature, not a bug.*
- *A floor plan is a memory palace.*
- *Costly symbols screen for loyalty.*

Deniable features

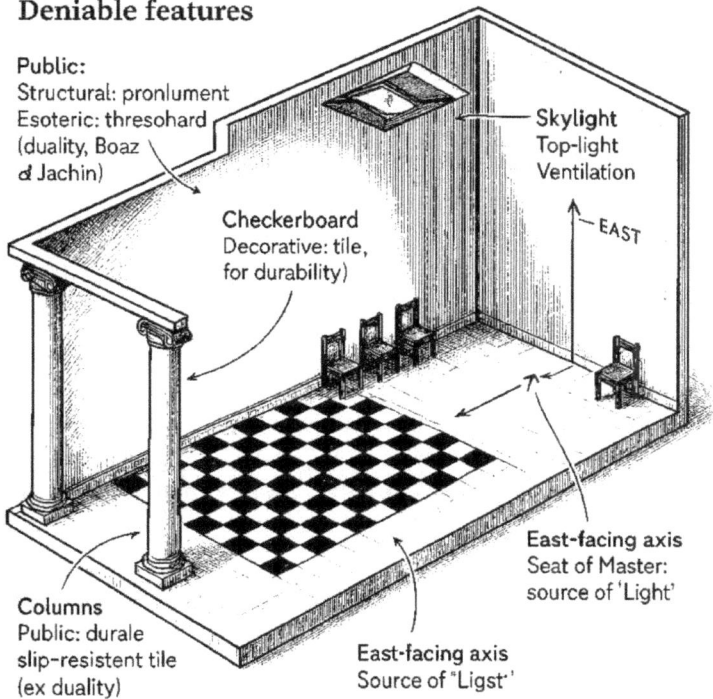

Public:
Structural: pronlument
Esoteric: thresohard
(duality, Boaz
d Jachin)

Skylight
Top-light
Ventilation

EAST

Checkerboard
Decorative: tile,
for durability)

East-facing axis
Seat of Master:
source of 'Light'

Columns
Public: durale
slip-resistent tile
(ex duality)

East-facing axis
Source of "Ligst''

The working grammar of symbols

Think of symbols not as a dictionary but as **grammar plus geometry**.
To read a façade, a seal, or a ritual route, investigate five layers:

- **Form:** Triangle, circle, square, spiral, vesica piscis, hexagram—
  the basic shapes with stable psychological effects (triangle =
  direction/priority; circle = unity/cycle; square = order/limit).

- **Number:** Counts of steps, columns, knots, petals, or stars.
  Three, five, seven, and nine are rarely accidental. Repetition is
  a sentence.

- **Orientation:** East/west alignments, left/right positioning (left = lunar/receptive; right = solar/active in many systems), above/below.

- **Sequence:** What you see or do first matters. Processions, knocks, or light changes are syntax.

- **Material/Color:** Black/white contrasts, gold leaf for the unaging, red for life-force or sacrifice, blue for firmament or wisdom. Stone type (granite, marble) can signal permanence or borrowed antiquity.

A single emblem usually supports **three concentric readings:**

- **Exoteric:** The public, harmless explanation ("decorative motif," "heritage pattern").

- **Mesoteric:** The fraternal or institutional reading (virtues, rank, chapter identity).

- **Esoteric:** The inner operational meaning (cosmology, method, oath-memory).

A Five-Minute Read of Any Building

1. *Count. How many of each feature? Any prime numbers?*
2. *Face it. Where does the main axis point? What greets the sunrise?*
3. *Layer the shapes. What shapes nest or intersect?*
4. *Follow the path. If you had to "walk the doctrine," where would your steps take you?*

Why do the same symbols reappear across millennia?

When you notice the same motifs—pillars guarding thresholds, the serpent biting its tail, the radiant sun disk, the eye within a triangle—your brain wants a single thriller plot to connect them. Sometimes there is lineage; often there is convergence. To separate romance from reality, apply this triage:

1. **Cognitive convergence.** Human eyes, hands, and environments are similar. Spirals (galaxies, shells, cyclones), grids (weaving, cities), and crosses (cardinal directions) are natural attractors.

2. **Trade routes and empire.** Motifs ride with merchants, captives, artisans, and mercenaries. A symbol that "leaps" cultures usually rode on a coin, a cloth pattern, or a portable amulet.

3. **Renaissance and revival.** Later groups deliberately mine antiquity for legitimacy. Reuse can be branding, not bloodline.

4. **Geometry doesn't age.** A triangle means hierarchy today for the same perceptual reasons it did two thousand years ago—one point is up, two are down.

A short field guide to recurrent motifs

Continuity or Coincidence?
Ask: (a) Is there a documented chain of contact? (b) Does the form carry the same meaning? (c) Is there evidence of deliberate revival? (d) Would human perception produce this shape anyway?

Use this catalogue not as gospel but as a set of working hypotheses:

- **Pillars/Twin columns:** Thresholds, duality, law/order vs. mercy/wisdom, gate to instruction. Placement at entrances signals passage from profane to initiated space.

- **Checkerboard floors:** A visual binary—light/dark, order/chaos—forcing spatial awareness and moral framing in each step.

- **Compass and square:** Measure and boundary; intangible intent (circle) calibrated by tangible constraint (square).

- **Spiral and labyrinth:** Path of descent and return; ordeal as pedagogy; time as a coil rather than a line.

- **Serpent forms:** Knowledge, danger, renewal (shedding skin), cyclicality (ouroboros).

- **Winged disk / radiant sun:** Sovereignty, legitimation "from above," cycles mastered.

- **Bees and honeycomb:** Industry, order, sweetness after discipline; sometimes linked to royal or priestly organization.

- **Keys:** Admission, withheld knowledge, jurisdiction; crossed keys imply binding/loosing authority.

- **Laurel and oak:** Victory/merit (laurel), endurance/virtue (oak).

- **Obelisk and dome:** Axis and vault—vertical aspiration paired with encompassing unity, often staged in urban pairs to dramatize heaven/earth dialogue.

- **Stars (five-point, six-point):** Human microcosm (five-point man), equilibrium of opposites (six-point interlaced triangles).

- **Handclasp and grip:** Covenant that pre-dates literacy; pact embodied.

Case files in stone: cities that speak

Some cities are lecture halls in plain sight. Three patterns recur:

1) Axial drama. Grand avenues frame ceremonial approaches to focal symbols (domes, arches, obelisks). Axes often align with solstices, equinoxes, or the ruler's preferred horizon. Whether by astronomical intent or aesthetic tradition, the result scripts light and movement.

2) Sacred pairs. An obelisk opposite a dome; twin towers bracketing a nave; a square opening to a round rotunda. The pairings teach duality-to-unity: boundary vs. embrace, law vs. grace, time vs. eternity.

3) The palimpsest. New regimes repurpose the last regime's symbols. Keep an eye on renamed squares, moved monuments, and "musealized" façades. Reuse is rarely neutral.

Be cautious with grand, single-cause claims (e.g., "the entire street grid was designed for one secret diagram"). Urban planning mixes aesthetics, topography, politics, and opportunism. Look for **local clusters** (a complex, a precinct, a single avenue) where meanings cohere and stewardship is traceable.

Ritual as embodied encryption

Ritual is a technology that writes doctrine into muscle memory. Entry is a threshold; veiling is a pedagogy; repetition is a compiler.

Core moves:

- **Orientation and light.** The candidate moves from obscurity to illumination, from west to east, from below to above. It's choreography with a doctrinal message: knowledge is earned, not handed over casually.

- **Threshold tests.** Knock counts, passwords, or tokens are less about secrecy than about rhythm and readiness. Getting the sequence right proves attention and humility.

- **Costliness.** Elaborate regalia, time-heavy rehearsals, and precise staging create a sunk-cost bond—group before self.

- **Witnessing.** Oaths are less legalese than social glue; the act of voicing binds the memory and marks the self.

Ethical note: Every legitimate fraternity understands that ritual without virtue is theater. Robust traditions pair inner work (character, charity, competence) with outer signs. Where spectacle displaces substance, symbols curdle into kitsch and power into coercion. The language still "works," but it speaks a degraded message.

Semiotics of power: money, seals, uniforms

If architecture is the slow speech of institutions, currency and seals are their crisp declarations. Ask three questions of any emblem on money, medals, or official stationery:

1. **Legitimation from where?** Crowns, halos, radiance, and mountaintop scenes imply top-down sanction.

2. **Power through what?** Tools (fasces, swords, scales, plow) reveal the institutional claim: order, justice, productivity.

3. **To what end?** Mottos—especially triads ("unity, order, progress"-type phrases)—broadcast the preferred virtues and the promised bargain with citizens or members.

Uniforms extend the same logic to bodies. Colors and cuts situate the wearer in a myth (knight, scholar, artisan, pilgrim), often with **hidden hierarchies** expressed through barely noticeable differences in fabric, stitching, or insignia placement. The paradox is the point: invisibility to outsiders, immediate legibility to insiders.

Case Study: The All-Seeing Eye Across Cultures

You've seen it everywhere—on temple reliefs, church paintings, banknotes, pop posters. It is the red thread through much of the modern suspicion around hidden orders. To understand the Eye, stop treating it as a single thing. It's a **family** of motifs that converged.

1) Eyes that protect vs. eyes that judge

Apotropaic eyes aim to ward off harm. The Mediterranean "evil eye" bead, blue and white, is a shield. The hamsa hand with an eye set in the palm is a deterrent: "I see you; move along." In this family, the eye is protective technology—human vigilance projected into an object.

Divine-witness eyes are about **conscience**. The eye framed by rays or set within a triangle telegraphs watcher-from-above: omniscience that makes deceit foolish. Medieval and early modern sacred art deployed this "Eye of Providence" to remind rulers and citizens that someone higher keeps the books. In this family, the eye enforces accountability.

Mystic-perception eyes (the "third eye" across South and East Asian traditions) signify inner sight—wisdom that sees through illusion. Here, the eye is a **capacity**, not surveillance.

2) Why the triangle?

Triangles concentrate attention. In Western sacred geometry, the triangle implies trinity/triune completeness; in craft traditions, it is simply the most stable shape. Placing the eye inside a triangle fuses **witness** (eye) with **order** (triangle). Rays add **glory**, implying the gaze emanates from beyond time. You don't need a conspiracy to explain why a new republic or a brotherhood seeking moral gravitas might adopt that package—it does the job efficiently.

3) How it moved and morphed

- **Temple warding and offerings.** Eye idols and votives in ancient shrines likely expressed both plea and presence: "I watch; please watch over me."

- **Sacred art codification.** As theological ideas about providence crystallized, artists standardized the eye-in-triangle with rays to teach omniscience visually.

- **State emblems.** New polities seeking virtue credentials borrowed the Eye of Providence to brand themselves as accountable to a higher standard.

- **Fraternal adoption.** Brotherhoods tasked with moral self-improvement and civic responsibility found in the eye-triangle a compact symbol for "no dark corners in the soul."

- **Pop culture remix.** In the twentieth and twenty-first centuries, mass media collapsed all these lines into a single high-contrast icon used ironically, ominously, or playfully. Meaning now depends on context more than origin.

4) How to read the Eye today without jumping at shadows

- **Context is king.** On a charity's seal? Likely conscience. On a satirical poster? Likely commentary on surveillance. In a ceremonial hall? Likely moral instruction.

- **Check the company it keeps.** Laurel (merit) vs. sword (coercion) vs. scales (justice) reframe the eye's tone.

- **Look for the practical corollary.** Are there policies, audits, or practices that match the "we are watched / we watch ourselves" claim? Symbols without practice are theater; practice without symbol is invisible culture.

Patterns, predictions, and the future of symbolic power

The medium is changing fast. Architecture still speaks, but new channels are noisier.

1) From stone to screen to stream

- **Logos as living sigils.** Modern marks are animated, reactive, and context-aware. They morph for event-specific versions (pride month palettes, climate campaigns), turning symbols into policy dashboards.

- **Memes as grassroots heraldry.** Online communities build their own sigils through repetition and remix. Watch for consistent color codes, mascots, and in-jokes evolving into serious markers of identity and influence.

- **AR layers on cities.** As augmented reality matures, power can mark space without touching stone. Expect "ceremonial overlays" visible only to credentialed devices on special days.

2) Steganography 2.0

Tiny glyphs in favicons, QR codes with "over-printing," and font ligatures can carry affiliation or permissions. The old tricks (acrostics, gematria) reappear in code comments, commit messages, and version numbers. The ritual isn't gone; it moved into developer culture.

3) Synthetic pattern storms

AI generates convincing faux-antique motifs and seals. Distinguishing **lineage** from **pastiche** will require provenance registers—an ironic return to illuminated charters, but now on blockchains. Hidden orders that care about authenticity will double down on verifiable craft (handcut stone, analog printing, hand-stitched regalia) precisely because it resists cheap replication.

4) Return of the oath

In an age of deepfakes and compromised feeds, the **embodied symbol**—witnessed commitments in physical spaces—becomes valuable again. Expect a rise in small-room rituals that leave no digital exhaust but create durable trust.

Your field notebook: reading without hallucinating

The more you notice, the more you're at risk of **apophenia**—finding patterns that aren't there. Investigators, not zealots, keep **null models** handy.

- **Start descriptive, end interpretive.** Count, map, sketch first. Only then ask "why."

- **Prefer clusters to isolates.** A single sunburst is designed; five coordinated sunbursts on a single axis under a shared patron deserve attention.

Five Predictions

- *AR will make "invisible architecture" a practical reality.*
- *Provenance tech will separate true tradition from AI-generated fog.*
- *Logos will act like dashboards, updating to show live values.*
- *Developer culture will host the next serious steganography.*
- *Small-room oaths will outperform large-room branding.*

- **Follow the money and maintenance.** Who pays for repairs? Who lights the candles and unlocks the doors? Living stewardship beats speculative origin stories.

- **Time-lock your claims.** Treat symbols as events in time. "This emblem meant X in 1820 and was reinterpreted as Y in 1920." Avoid timeless claims; symbols live.

- **Check the boring documents.** Permits, dedication speeches, donor lists. Often, the "secret" is hiding in the minutes that nobody reads.

Bringing Part I and Part V into one sightline

From ancient roots to future patterns, continuity is not a magic tunnel beneath history; it is a braided river. The banks shift; the channels split. Yet the water keeps heading seaward:

- The **Stone Age spiral** resurfaces in initiation mazes and corporate logos because spirals compress movement and time into a single glance.

- The **pillared threshold** returns in data-center entrances because guardianship rituals adapt to new treasure (information instead of grain).

- The **eye that once warded off envy** now signals accountability in institutions that proclaim they are watched by auditors, citizens, or God.

Hidden orders, whether monastic, mercantile, military, or civic, have worked with a consistent toolkit: geometry, number, direction, and repetition. That toolkit survives because it maps to human bodies and minds. As the stage shifts from queries to code, the same grammar now scripts apps, dashboards, badges, and AR scenes. The symbols won't vanish; they will **refactor.**

Treat every symbol like a witness. Ask what it saw, what it wants you to feel, and who benefits if you agree. There is romance in the chase, but the payoff is practical: better reading of institutions, quicker detection of theater, and a steadier compass when rumor thickens the air. The language of symbols is not mystical fog—it is a field manual. Learn the grammar, keep your head, walk the route, and you will hear the quiet orders that outlast the loud ones.

Chapter 14

Do Secret Societies Control Human Destiny?

You opened this file because you want straight answers to a loaded question—and you want them told like a seasoned investigator would tell a trusted partner. So let's make a pact: I'll neither sensationalize nor sanitize. We'll look at what's alleged, what's documented, and what actually moves outcomes in the real world. We'll also keep a running eye on *how* secrecy itself creates leverage—sometimes decisive leverage—even when no one is pulling puppet strings.

To do that properly, we'll separate spectacle from substance. Conspiracy folklore often hands you an all-powerful cabal orchestrating history like a symphony. Reality is messier: overlapping networks, competing ambitions, rituals that bind insiders, and closed-door forums that *shape the menu* of options long before anything hits the public diary. That's where influence becomes durable. When the menu is set, choosing the dish is a formality.

Before we dive into famous names, let's fix our definitions.

Control is when a clandestine group can impose outcomes at will.

Influence is when a group can narrow choices, coordinate narratives, fast-track allies, or slow-roll adversaries—without guaranteeing the end state.

History has vastly more of the second than the first.

Theories vs. Documented Influence

We'll test the strongest claims against records from real institutions—some with ritual and myth, others with bare, fluorescent lighting and keycard doors. The yardstick is simple: What can we verify about who meets, what they do inside, and what changes on the outside?

Closed-door elite forums: high signal, soft power

The Bilderberg conference is the canonical example of a private forum whose attendees—heads of government, finance, defense, and industry—don't need a fantasy plotline to be consequential. The origin story is prosaic: a 1954 gathering at the Hotel de Bilderberg in the Netherlands, catalyzed by political fixer Jozef Retinger (a wartime operator who once parachuted into Nazi-occupied Poland) and front-chaired by Prince Bernhard. The group centralized around a steering committee; attendance hovered around ~120 invite-only "heavy hitters," and the posture was tight-lipped: a minimalist mailbox in Leiden, a pamphlet to keep up appearances, and a brief press release and attendee list around each meeting. That's enough opacity to breed rumors, and enough caliber to make those rumors plausible to outsiders.

What about outcomes? Critics point to figures like Clinton and Blair who rose shortly after attending, waving this as proof of orchestration. A cooler reading is that Bilderberg scouts momentum and convenes people already set to ascend. Think talent aggregation and consensus

The Big Distinction
Control = *command over outcomes.*
Influence = *command over options. Watch who writes the options list; they're often the ones "shaping destiny."*

formation—not a master switchboard. The real influence is atmospheric: getting senior players to converge around what is "responsible," "inevitable," or "off the table." That sort of convergence can tilt policy landscapes without a single vote being cast.

Religious orders with rumor-magnets: aura vs. apparatus

Some organizations acquire a mystique that outruns their actual structure. Opus Dei is a case study in this gap. It's a personal prelature within the Catholic Church with strict discipline and old-fashioned ascetic practices (e.g., the thigh-worn cilice), which outsiders read as sinister. But the plain portrait is of a pious, hierarchical body distrusted mainly because it swims upstream against secular culture, not because it's a world-dominating murder cult. The secrecy here is the "discretion of a private association," not an underworld command center. In short: more aura than apparatus.

University "tombs" and the leadership pipeline: networks are the asset

Yale's senior societies—Skull and Bones, Scroll and Key, Wolf's Head, and others—are not national command posts. They are high-octane social engines that bind small cohorts (often fifteen per year) through ritual, shared confessions, odd traditions (clocks set five minutes fast, "Bones time"), and deep alumni patronage. Over time, that mix creates a preferential highway into elite careers—media, law, intelligence, finance, politics. Influence arises not from issuing orders but from network density and trust: who you can call at midnight, and who returns the call.

State secrecy and "shadow government": continuity beats conspiracy

If you want a glimpse of "destiny handling," skip the lodges and look at bunkers. Mount Weather and the broader Federal Relocation Arc exist to keep the U.S. government running after decapitation events—nuclear exchange, mass attack, or widespread infrastructure collapse. The details are unromantic and very real: underground command spaces, duplicate departmental chains, living quarters for thousands, and hardened communications. People remembered 9/11 for the visible events; power professionals remember it for the invisible relocations that proved the apparatus works. This isn't a society; it's a *system*—and systems shape outcomes by pre-defining continuity.

> **The Quietest Power**
> Continuity infrastructure doesn't pass laws; it ensures there's always someone around to pass them tomorrow. That's not a conspiracy; it's a structural veto on chaos.

Occultized ideology inside a police state: when ritual operationalizes violence

The SS's Wewelsburg project—a "Black Camelot" with a crypt below and a ritual hall above—was not a gentleman's club; it was a cult architecture wrapped around a lethal bureaucracy. The black-sun mosaic, a circle of twelve seats, and invented heraldry served a grim purpose: to re-sacramentalize ritual loyalty and moral anesthesia before campaigns that included mass murder. The castle functioned as a symbolic center that fused mythology with orders, using ceremony to harden the conscience against ordinary scruples. That is a *documented* influence of the deadliest kind: ritual as a tool for operational brutality.

Why Secrecy Itself Wields Power

Whether we're discussing a boarding-school tomb, a corporate-government forum, a religious order, or a state bunker, secrecy confers advantages. These aren't mystic; they're practical.

1. **Information asymmetry.** Decisions formed without public negotiation face less resistance. If the first time a policy is "public" is after elites have stabilized around it, opposition is robbed of time and coordination. (Think of the annual private convergence at Bilderberg creating a "reasonable center" that then shows up in speeches and editorials.)

2. **Bonding under ritual strain.** Confession circles and odd rites look theatrical from the outside, but they produce durable trust. Bones-style "life story" disclosures and disorienting initiations turn classmates into confidants; confidants grease future deals.

3. **Status signaling.** If you're "in the room," you must be worth hearing—an unspoken credential that travels into hiring,

appointments, and briefings. Yale tombs and elite conclaves signal membership in a tribe of deciders.

4. **Narrative discipline.** Groups with internal taboos and shared myths maintain message coherence. That discipline is rocket fuel inside politics and media cycles. (You can see the dark extreme at Wewelsburg, where myth-saturated orders to dissolve empathy.)

5. **Deniability.** When minutes aren't published and attendees are bound by non-attribution, claims of "no official decisions" are technically true—while the practical effect is collective alignment.

How Policy Consensus Is Manufactured

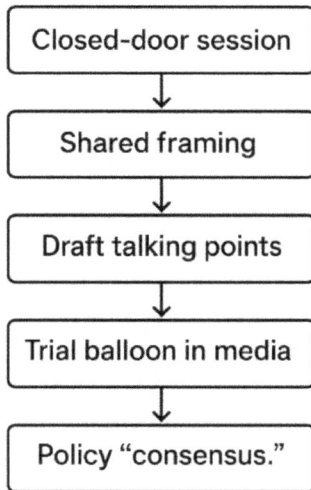

```
┌─────────────────────────┐
│   Closed-door session   │
└─────────────────────────┘
             ↓
┌─────────────────────────┐
│     Shared framing      │
└─────────────────────────┘
             ↓
┌─────────────────────────┐
│  Draft talking points   │
└─────────────────────────┘
             ↓
┌─────────────────────────┐
│  Trial balloon in media │
└─────────────────────────┘
             ↓
┌─────────────────────────┐
│   Policy "consensus."   │
└─────────────────────────┘
```

Case Studies: Outcomes vs. Alleged Agendas

Let's put the claims on trial: side-by-side, allegation vs. verifiable effect.

Case A — Bilderberg: From "World Directorate" to "Consensus Factory"

Allegation: It's a supranational directorate placing leaders and issuing marching orders.

Record we can see: Established 1954; curated invite list; minimal formal structure; short public communiqués; no binding resolutions. The attendee universe includes future heads of government and top corporate and central-bank officials. The same names later show up executing the "reasonable middle" on trade, integration, and security matters. That looks like elite alignment, not central planning. The Clinton/Blair timing is better explained by recruitment to *emerging consensus* than by secret coronation rites.

Result: High influence on *which* choices are framed as viable; low evidence of unilateral command.

Takeaway: Destiny isn't dictated; it's *bound.* The power is in shrinking public debate.

Case B — Wewelsburg and the SS: When Esoteric Theater Becomes Administrative Violence

Allegation: Occult orders are just cosplay.

Records we can see: The SS turned ritual space into an instrument of moral re-engineering: a tomb-like crypt below, a myth-charged hall above, a ring of "knights," invented coats of arms, and a black-sun emblem. Speeches given there aligned cadres before invasions and extermination programs. The castle's cult did not *cause* the Holocaust; it helped *normalize* the perpetrators to do it. That's not theater; that's weaponized ritual.

Result: Ritual amplified atrocity by stripping inhibitors and sacralizing orders.

Takeaway: Secrecy plus myth can widen the zone of the "permissible"—sometimes catastrophically.

Case C — Yale Senior Societies: Ritual → Network → Placement

Allegation: Bones "runs America."

Records we can see: The societies are small cohorts that ritualize trust, seed reciprocal favors, and maintain alumni corridors across journalism, finance, law, intel, and politics. Bones' oddities (five-minute-fast clocks; life-story disclosures) are cohesion tools. Over decades, this network effect yields *access* and *acceleration*, not command lines. Even insider ratings once ribbed Bones for "peculiarity" and "exclusivity" more than raw "power."

Result: Nontrivial influence through trust-dense networking; no evidence of national-level control.

Takeaway: The myth of omnipotence confuses *who knows whom* with *who rules what.*

Case D — Continuity Networks: The System That Outranks Every Secret Society

Allegation: "Shadow government" bunkers are proof of hidden rulers.
Records we can see: Continuity sites like Mount Weather existed long before the current conspiracist vocabulary and are openly described (in broad strokes) as infrastructure to sustain constitutional government under attack. After 9/11, their activity and upgrades were observable

in localities and planning records. There's nothing mystical here; it's conscious redundancy—a wiring diagram for the republic.

Result: The apparatus shapes destiny by preventing power vacuums. **Takeaway:** If you're looking for a "hidden hand," sometimes it's a reinforced blast door.

The Patterns: How "Hidden Orders" Actually Shape the Future

Put these cases on one screen, and the pattern sharpens.

1. **Gatekeeping beats diktat.** Across elites, the decisive lever is pre-selection of people, frames, and policies. Bilderberg's value is who's *framed in*. Yale tombs' value is in who's *brought along*. Gatekeeping looks polite on the surface; it's ruthless under the hood.

2. **Ritual compresses hesitation.** From benign "tell-all" nights to the SS's lethal liturgy, ritual's job is always the same: reduce friction inside the group so the group can move as one.

> ### Reader's Field Test (Use This in Real Time)
>
> *When a rumor claims control, test for: (1) Coercive capacity (or just prestige?), (2) Repeatable mechanisms (or one-off spectacle?), (3) Observed policy shifts within 3–18 months of the gathering.*

3. **Secrecy is a time advantage.** Private convergence gives months of a head start on public debate. By the time the talk-show panels wake up, the middle has moved.

4. **Infrastructure quietly outranks ideology.** You can swap out leaders and parties; you cannot swap out hardened continuity systems in a crisis. The wiring wins.

5. **Myth markets.** Stories—of sacred lineage, special destiny, "chosen peers"—sell cohesion. Sometimes that's merely clubby; sometimes it lubricates cruelty. Knowing which is which is the historian's first duty.

Why People Believe in Total Control (and Why That Matters)

It would be easy to mock grand theories of total control, but their popularity tells us something: modern life often feels pre-decided. People sense that debates are scripted, choices are cosmetic, and big calls happen elsewhere. They're not wrong to feel that. The "elsewhere" is real: **agenda-setting** in elite forums, **pipeline curation** in selective networks, **myth-fueled** inside ideological orders, and **continuity design** inside state infrastructure.

The mistake is leaping from *bounded choices* to *total control*. The bounds are nudged by real actors using secrecy to coordinate without interference. They succeed enough to matter, and fail often enough to prove they're not gods.

Practical Tools: Reading the Next Decade

Here's how to watch the ground beneath public politics.

Follow the conveners, not the headlines. Identify the two or three recurring off-camera gatherings that seat people across finance, defense, energy, and tech. They won't publish minutes, but they do publish attendee lists or venue habits. Track the vocabulary that leaks out—often bland phrases like "resilience," "harmonization," or "responsible innovation." That vocabulary is the tell for where consensus is drifting.

Map pipelines. Don't ask "Is there a cabal?" Ask "Where do cohorts bond before they're visible?" Campus societies, clerkship patterns, think-tank fellowships, and boutique finance apprenticeships are the pipelines. An outsize share of tomorrow's officials and editors will know each other from those rooms.

Interrogate rituals. When a group treats its internal rites like a sacrament, it's telling you cohesion outranks dissent. That's either a high-trust incubator or a moral hazard—context decides. From awkward confessional circles to choreographed black-sun symbolism, ritual signals how far a group will go to keep members on script.

Respect the wiring diagram. In any upheaval, ask: what continuity systems kick in? Those systems are destiny's guardrails. They decide who can declare emergencies, sign orders, and keep satellites whispering.

Chapter 15

The Choice Before Us

We've reached the point in the investigation where the complicated gives way to the simple: there is a pattern to how hidden orders work, there is a pattern to how they maintain influence, and there is a pattern to how they are challenged and—sometimes—replaced. The question is not whether these patterns exist. The question is what we decide to do with them.

I'll keep this grounded, practical, and focused on what matters now. You've seen how sanctuaries—monasteries and fortresses, boardrooms and bank vaults, tunnels and islands—give cover for coordination. You've seen how symbols—rings, emblems, relics, passwords—activate belonging. You've seen how rituals—oaths, feasts, duels, quiet handshakes—convert loose circles into durable networks. And you've seen that secrecy isn't just about hiding; it's about pacing when and how power becomes visible.

This chapter takes those threads and ties them off. First, can humanity break free of hidden orders? Second, why does exposing secrets rarely change much on its own? And third, how to read the long pattern of power without falling for either mythmaking or fatalism.

Can humanity break free of hidden orders?

Short answer: not from the human impulse that creates them. But we can change their **shape, scope,** and **accountability**.

Hidden orders aren't an alien implant; they're a feature of group life under scarcity and risk. When outside pressure rises—war, plague, financial panic—people cluster, and a cluster needs rules. If danger is acute, those rules move inward, away from public view. That's how you get sanctuaries and bolt-holes, from medieval priest holes to modern continuity-of-government hubs. The architectural details change; the logic doesn't. The tunnel popes used to escape mobs, the emergency centers meant to outlast a nuclear blast, the desert test site that "doesn't exist" on a map—all express the same instinct: preserve a core, then rebuild from it.

At the same time, orders that begin as defensive shells often become offensive launchpads. The chapel, the club, the lodge, the "temporary" committee—each can evolve into a place where insiders set agendas for everyone else. Elite student societies, for example, aren't powerful because of one spooky ceremony; they're powerful because they bond people early, across decades, across sectors. That is succession planning disguised as collegiate nostalgia.

So "breaking free" is the wrong metaphor if it imagines a purity that never existed. The workable ambition is narrower and more radical: **replace opaque monopolies with constrained, plural networks** and **force any sanctuary that shapes public outcomes to submit to public rules.** Not a world with no hidden rooms—humans will always build rooms—but a world where no single locked room can decide everyone's fate.

Why exposing secrets may not be enough

What "breaking free" really means
- *Aim to **limit monopoly** (no network gets a permanent lock on the future).*
- *Impose **accountable secrecy** (some operations can be shielded; none can be unreviewable).*
- *Build **rival centers of competence** (so one order's failure doesn't become everyone's catastrophe).*

In every era, reformers think that sunlight is the solvent. Reveal the minutes, leak the membership list, publish the map—job done. And yes, disclosures matter. They puncture myths. They strip away the aura that secrecy alone can grant. But too often the aftershock is disappointment: little changes.

Why? Because power is **not** co-extensive with information. Power rests in **capability, coordination**, and **switching costs**. If a hidden order controls a logistics chain, a treasury desk, a recruitment funnel, or a crisis bunker, publishing its phone book doesn't dissolve any of that. The risk-reducing functions remain. The exit costs remain. So the network can absorb the scandal and keep going.

This is why a sanctuary can be "exposed" and yet become more influential—counterintuitive, but common. Once the mystique is gone, what remains is its **utility**. If the network is useful (or feared), stakeholders will re-normalize the relationship. Think of government bolt-holes and signals intelligence sites: outing them didn't end them; it professionalized them. The facilities endured because the capabilities they house—continuity, early warning, strategic research—are not optional in a high-risk world.

The same dynamic applies to historic spiritual-political hubs. Wewelsburg, for instance, shows how a theatrical mythology can be wrapped around a core of brutal capability; dismantling the pageantry doesn't erase the organizational techniques that were learned there. The lesson isn't to romanticize it (we shouldn't), but to recognize how **ritual plus mission** locks people to a cause. Exposure without alternative loyalties leaves the structure intact.

And then there is **supply and demand**. People want places to belong, to be initiated, to "matter." Remove one secret room without creating healthier rooms, and the demand simply finds a different door. This is why "naming and shaming" works best when paired with **substitution**—new pathways into careers, different sources of status, backup infrastructures that make the old gatekeepers optional. Elite student societies only dominate when we let them monopolize **first-name basis** access to future bosses. Break that pipeline with rival fellowships and transparent mentorship exchanges, and the magnetism changes.

Anatomy of a hidden order (the neutral model)

To act wisely, we need a neutral, non-mythic model—one that applies to a medieval order, a twentieth-century strategic bunker, and a present-day executive network just the same. Strip away aesthetics; keep the mechanics:

1. **Sanctuary (Place).** A protected space—physical or digital—where members meet without interruption, store sensitive materials, and ride out shocks. It can be overt (a private club on a famous street) or deniable (a "doesn't exist" facility). It reduces exposure and synchronizes the group's tempo.

2. **Symbol (Signal).** A token, crest, relic, phrase, or gesture that compresses the group's identity. It's a memory device and a filter: those who misuse it or don't react to it are outside. Symbols can be ancient (a crowned relic) or engineered (a modern logo for a continuity agency).

3. **Script (Ritual).** A repeatable sequence—oath, meal, chant, ceremony, duel, or, today, a standard onboarding—designed to bind members and transmit norms. The content can be uplifting or appalling; the function is the same: commitment through memorized action.

4. **Switchboard (Network).** The actual value: names, roles, favors, a route to money, security, or time. This is the "quiet switchboard" that allocates scarce opportunities. Historic versions might include an island monastery's scriptorium or a

banker's salon; modern versions are spreadsheets, encrypted chats, and alumni breakfasts.

5. **Story (Narrative).** A theory of the world that makes the group's existence feel necessary. When the story is convincing, members will defend the order as if defending reality itself.

Put those five together and you have something that resists accidents and absorbs scrutiny. If one pillar is attacked (say, the symbol is mocked), the others hold.

Replication: how hidden orders reproduce themselves

Think of this as **elite biology.** Orders propagate through:

- **Patronage:** Old members place new members in roles that matter. Over time, this becomes an inheritance system.

- **Annexation:** The order wraps itself around an external capability—a library, a bank, a regiment, a lab. Control the asset, and you control the funnel of talent that flows through it.

- **Myth maintenance:** A compelling story deters defections, even when returns drop. Rituals turn sunk costs into a badge of honor.

- **Emergency utility:** Crises legitimize hidden rooms. After a shock, the group that can convene, decide, and move gets de facto sovereignty.

You saw many versions of this earlier: a tunnel that made popes mobile; an airfield and test range that made a program possible; a seed vault that made a species of plant survivable; a bank parlor that made capital move discreetly; a senior society meeting room that made careers cohere. Different aesthetics, same Darwinian pressures.

> **Replication checklist**
>
> *If you observe patronage + asset control + ritual + crisis utility, you're looking at a self-reproducing order—even if it denies being one.*

Breaking points: where hidden orders actually fail

Orders don't die because someone blogs their handshake. They die when one of four things happens:

A. The sanctuary loses scarcity. If a place once guaranteed privacy and now everyone has equivalent privacy on their phone—or drones can see through the roof—the advantage devalues. The order must either harden (expensive) or transform (hard).

B. The switchboard is bypassed. New channels—open capital markets, public grant platforms, transparent promotion tracks—make the old gatekeepers optional. When exit costs drop, loyalty is renegotiated.

C. The story collapses from results. When outcomes consistently contradict the narrative (e.g., promised moral superiority followed by obvious abuses), members defect in silence. The order might persist as a costume but loses decisive capacity.

D. The risk landscape flips. If the order was designed for one kind of crisis (say, a Cold War exchange) and the world pivots to different threats (say, cyber-financial cascades), the old sanctuary becomes a liability. That's when rival centers grow.

Note the pattern: **capability changes**, not just information changes. That's why your strategy should be capability-centric too.

The practical protocols (individual and civic)

If exposing secrets is insufficient, what works? You need **protocols**—repeatable moves that alter capability, coordination, and costs.

Individual protocols

Protocol 1: Build multi-affiliation lives. The best personal defense against a single order's gravity is diversified belonging. Be part of overlapping communities—technical, artistic, civic—that don't owe each other favors. Then no single switchboard can punish you cheaply.

Protocol 2: Practice "quiet transparency." Document interactions that could be twisted later—what was promised, what was delivered—without grandstanding. Quiet records are what let truth survive beyond cycles of hype and outrage.

Protocol 3: Replace cynical voyeurism with constructive curiosity. Don't collect secrets as trophies. Learn enough about an order's real function (finance, research, logistics, safety) to create or join a substitute. Curiosity becomes capability.

Protocol 4: Rituals of integrity. Make your own micro-rituals—how you open a project, how you close one—so that the "script" that binds you isn't someone else's oath you never agreed to.

Organizational & civic protocols

Protocol A: Constrained sanctuaries. Allow for genuinely private rooms—journalist source protection, cabinet strategy sessions, R&D labs—but wrap them in legal and technical guardrails: independent audits, after-action disclosures, renewable secrecy warrants, rotation of oversight bodies. The facility endures; the **unreviewability** does not. Think of how exposed government sites evolved into professionalized, overseen installations without ceasing to exist.

Protocol B: Redundancy by design. Don't let a single order own the only working version of something society can't live without (payments, identity, emergency communications, seed stocks). Build a **federation** of alternatives, with standard interfaces, so switches are cheap when a hub fails.

Protocol C: Open succession ladders. Replace insider pipelines with open competitions for scholarships, apprenticeships, and public-interest residencies. That's how you reduce the career premium that a secret dining room still confers. The aim is not to humiliate the old network; it is to make **opting out** painless.

Protocol D: Myth hygiene. Separate two questions: "Is there a sanctum?" and "Is it supernatural?" Hidden rooms are normal; magical explanations are optional. Treat the first with documentation, the second with disciplined doubt. You end up neither credulous nor blind.

Protocol E: Crisis rehearsals for the public. Don't leave continuity drills to insiders only. Cities and regions can run transparent, civil-led simulations for food, water, cash, and communications shocks. When the public can self-organize, the monopoly on emergency legitimacy erodes.

Case studies revisited, with the new lens.

Let's pressure-test the model against familiar sites and orders—not to retell their history, but to extract what actually matters for the choices in front of us.

The escape corridor and the crisis mandate. A hidden passage in the heart of an empire gave leaders proof they could outlast street violence. That corridor wasn't just stone; it was a promise of continuity. Today's equivalents are hardened data centers and emergency operation hubs. The accountability move isn't demolition; it's **conditional legitimacy**—they're allowed **because** their use is reviewable.

The "doesn't exist" facility and capability candor. A test range that denies itself on paper can still become a public legend. When the myth fog clears, the center of gravity remains: advanced prototyping out of the public eye. The grown-up stance is not to pretend we can run all R&D in the town square, but to insist on guardrails whose breach has consequences.

The fortress of ideology and ritualized loyalty. A gothic stronghold once married pageantry to policy, creating a template for fanatical obedience. The countermeasure isn't merely debunking the costumes; it is **competing loyalties** that channel commitment into life-preserving missions. Ritual isn't going away. Better rituals must exist.

Elite student rooms and the quiet switchboard. A handful of societies organize future leaders with dinners, archives, and an address book. Instead of fantasy-busting only, build rival programs that give a 19-year-old the same first-call access to future collaborators—without the lifetime obligation to a sealed room. **Replace the switchboard, don't just expose it.**

The bank parlor and the power of discretion. Private banking thrives because some clients want discretion and craftsmanship. Demonizing discretion doesn't end it; professionalizing and supervising it does. The threshold question becomes: **When does private discretion spill into public risk?** When it does, the sanctuary must accept shared rules or lose its charter.

INSTITUTIONS: THEN & NOW
(Monochrome Montage)

| Ancient passage | Desert runway | Black-stone castle | Ivy door with crest |
| Modern ops room | Black project sillouettes | humanitarian ops center | Regulator dashboard |

The emotional core: why people join, why they stay, why they leave

We can get lost in structure and forget the human layer. People join hidden orders for three reasons in combination:

- **Competence:** The order gets things done and teaches you how.

- **Camaraderie:** These are your people; the rituals make that bond feel real.

- **Coverage:** The order shields you—career cover, legal cover, physical cover—in a chaotic world.

They stay when those three are strong and costs are low. They leave when capability falls, when the ritual turns empty or abusive, or when cheaper, cleaner coverage appears elsewhere.

Here's the awkward truth: the solution to unhealthy orders is **better orders**, not no orders. Humans need rooms. The choice is whether those rooms are **bounded and pro-social**, or **totalizing and predatory**. That's not cynicism; that's design.

Learning from the patterns of power (final reflection)

By now, the patterns should be visible without decoration:

- **Sanctuary** concentrates on coordination.

- **Symbol** encodes identity.

- **Script** imprints loyalty.

- **Switchboard** dispenses advantage.

- **Story** creates meaning.

Everything else is commentary or costume.

From the ancient sancta where relics were guarded to modern sanctuaries where data and decision-rights are stored, the through-line is continuity under pressure. An island monastery safeguarded faith and manuscripts. A modern Arctic vault safeguards biodiversity. A fortified castle turned wicked when its story and script fused with a politics of extermination. A private bank parlor steered fortunes across centuries. A tunnel once saved a pontiff; an underground Continuity of Government grid is meant to save an administration. A university society turns acquaintances into a life-long "we." The names and myths differ; the mechanics rhyme.

So the real "choice before us" is painfully specific:

1. **Which capabilities must sanctuaries have?** Food resilience, medical stockpiles, communications continuity, secure archives—these deserve protected rooms. Make them **plural and overseen**.

2. **Which sanctuaries must never be sovereign?** Any room that claims to rule without consent or review—no matter how ancient its crest or how modern its card reader.

3. **How do we keep rituals humane?** Encourage meaning-making that binds people to care and competence, not to cruelty and domination.

4. **How do we cheapen the cost of exit?** Scholarships, grants, second-chance hiring, interoperable credentials—every time you make exit cheaper, you reduce the leverage of monopolistic rooms.

5. **What legacy do we accept?** Not all relics are talismans; some are warnings. Treat the worst as hazard signs, not treasure maps. Treat the best as blueprints for service: places that preserve without preying.

Can we actually do this?

Yes, because we already do, in pieces. Consider these closing realities drawn from our tour:

- Secret places that began as improvised corridors now operate as maintained public assets with oversight. That's what institutionalization looks like when it's done right.

- Facilities that were once rumor-only are now professional programs with budgets and inspectors; they remain selective and shielded, but not lawless. Oversight hasn't killed capability; it has often increased it.

- Elite rooms still confer an edge, but their monopoly is soft. Where rival ladders exist—open fellowships, transparent hiring, public-service corps—the private crest loses its chokehold.

- Treasured totems and shrines still inspire, but the better lesson isn't to worship artifacts; it's to study what they **enabled**—records kept safe, communities fed, wisdom transmitted—and fund those functions in ways that do not require an oath of silence.

This isn't utopia. It's disciplined pluralism under stress.

A practical reading guide for patterns

When you encounter a new story about an order or site—ancient relics in a chapel, a desert base with odd lights, an island with a treasure legend, a club with an unwritten code—ask five questions:

1. **What capability is actually being preserved here?** If you can't name it, you're dealing with a myth-shell. If you can, assess whether that capability deserves protection and on what terms.

(Example: escape corridors that secure governance; seed vaults that secure biodiversity.)

2. **Who controls the switchboard?** Is access to money, records, safety, or careers centralized? Who can audit it? Without an audit trail, you have unreviewable sovereignty disguised as tradition.

3. **What are the exit costs?** If leaving the order costs you reputation, income, or safety, a reform agenda must start by lowering those costs. Build backups before you blow whistles.

4. **What crisis does the narrative claim to solve?** If the crisis is real, offer a cleaner fix. If it's imagined, the order's power may be performative—loud but brittle.

5. **Where are the interfaces to the public?** Healthy sanctuaries have doors that open—after-action reports, rotating oversight, expiration of secrecy, and appeal processes.

Apply those five, and you won't get lost in either the romance or the panic.

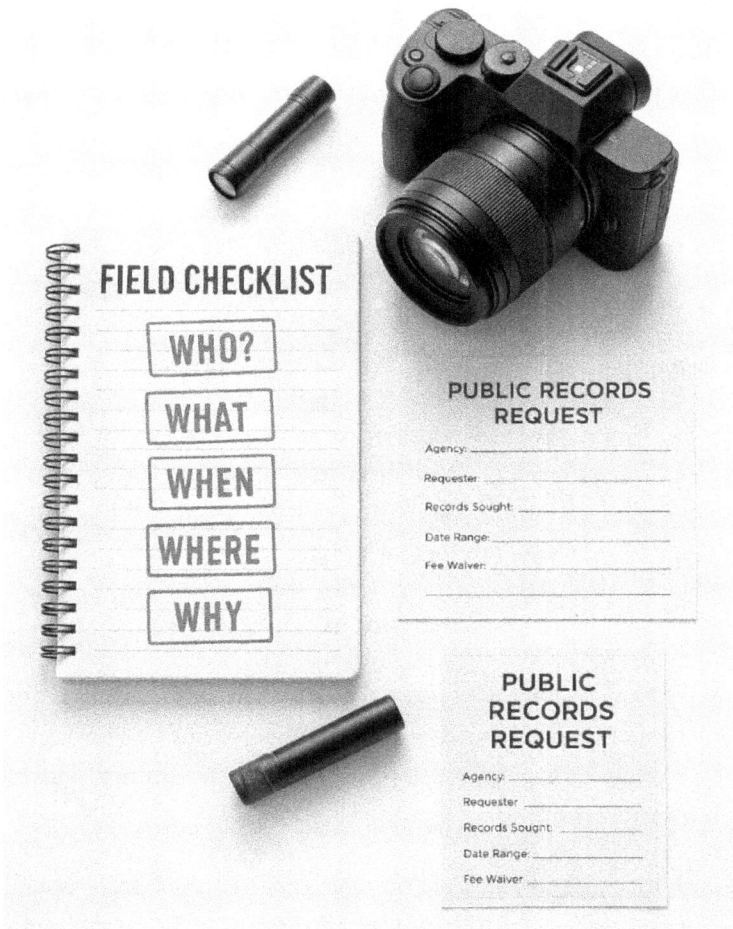

FIELD CHECKLIST

WHO?
WHAT
WHEN
WHERE
WHY

PUBLIC RECORDS REQUEST

Agency: _____
Requester: _____
Records Sought: _____
Date Range: _____
Fee Waiver: _____

PUBLIC RECORDS REQUEST

Agency: _____
Requester: _____
Records Sought: _____
Date Range: _____
Fee Waiver: _____

The future: pattern shifts you should expect

The next sanctuary won't always be stone; it will be **compute**. Expect the switchboard to be partly algorithmic, the symbol to be partly a keypair, and the script to be a smart contract. That doesn't mean the pattern ends; it means it migrates. Your job remains the same: constrain monopolies, multiply capable rooms, and keep public outcomes under public rules.

We will also see **hybrid sanctuaries**: physical sites with digital shadows—emergency centers mirrored in cloud regions; private archives mirrored in distributed storage; closed-door deliberations mirrored by legally required "decision dossiers" that publish within a year.

And the new crisis is not only bombs and bank runs; it's **systemic cascades**—supply chains, grids, and info-spheres failing in synchrony. The rooms that can dampen cascades will claim legitimacy. Build **federations** now so that no single room owns the fuse box.

Finally, the most precious capability to preserve is not a relic or a runway. It's **trustworthy coordination among strangers**. Hidden orders are an old way to do that. We can do better, in the open enough to be fair, in the private enough to be safe.

The choice before us (final words)

The choice is not whether sanctuaries exist. They will. The choice is whether we let a few rooms harden into private sovereignties—or whether we insist on a world with **many rooms, many routes, and rules that reach them all**.

We honor the best of the past by rescuing its functions—continuity, craft, courage—from the worst of its monopolies. We strip cruel scripts of their glamour and replace them with rituals that bind people to service, not subservience. We stop worshiping emblems and start funding capabilities that keep communities alive. We don't build a world with no secrets; we build a world where secrets **serve** the public, not the other way around.

If you want a single sentence to carry out of this chapter, use this:

Any room that sets public outcomes must accept public rules.

Say it in a castle, in a club, in a cabinet, in a data center. Then act as if it's already the law of the land—and help write the laws that make it true.

Bonus Section: Hidden Orders Workbook

Let's treat this as your field kit—the practical, nuts-and-bolts companion to the book. The pages that follow are designed to help you map patterns, decode symbols, cross-check claims, and keep your head clear when the noise gets loud. Use it actively: annotate, underline, sketch. The aim isn't to collect trivia; it's to train your eye and judgment so you can read power in two layers at once—the public theater and the quiet choreography behind it.

Orientation: The Five Moves You'll Practice

Before we jump into timelines and symbol decks, lock in five basic moves. They're simple, repeatable, and they keep you honest.

1. **Name the capability.** For any secretive group or site, ask: *What useful capability is being preserved or coordinated here?* (Money? Records? Recruitment? Crisis continuity? Dissent?) If you can't name a capability, you're staring at branding, not power.

2. **Locate the sanctuary.** Where is the protected space—physical or digital—where coordination happens? How is access controlled? What are the thresholds, and who guards them?

3. **Track the calendar.** When do key meetings or announcements cluster? Do they rhyme with feast days, anniversaries, initiatory seasons, or predictable offsite cycles?

4. **Follow the switchboard.** What relationships actually move outcomes—letters of introduction, private dinners, alumni circles, discreet bankers, shadow negotiating channels?

5. **Measure exit costs.** If members leave, what do they lose? If critics speak up, what happens? Low exit costs mean competitive openness; high exit costs mean leverage.

Timeline of Major Secret Orders and Their Influence

This isn't an exhaustive catalogue; it's a backbone you can hang details on. The goal is to feel continuity—how forms of secrecy adapt to new regimes while preserving their core mechanics: sanctuary, ritual, continuity. Keep the summaries tight, then expand with your own notes.

✓ Antiquity (c. 2000 BCE – 300 CE)

Temple-Schools & Omen Guilds (Egypt & Mesopotamia). What mattered: ritualized custodianship of calendars, medicine, law, and state advice. Knowledge was gated through oaths, purity codes, and apprenticeship. Influence flowed because accuracy and timing were survival skills.

Influence move: Turn astronomy and liturgy into policy language; bind kings and cities to the specialists who "read" the cosmos.

Mystery Rites (Eleusis, Dionysiac, Isis).

What mattered: graded initiation; controlled sensory experiences that imprinted belonging and promised moral renewal. Often co-managed with civic authorities.

Influence move: Use secrecy to protect transformative rites; use the rites to stabilize social identity and political loyalty.

Philosophical-Religious Schools (Pythagoreans, Hermetic circles). What mattered: inner teachings behind public texts, strict discipline, a rhetoric of rebirth.

Influence move: Train small elites in shared vocabulary and habitus that later travel into law, finance, and governance.

✓ Late Antiquity & Early Medieval (c. 300–1100)

Monastic Networks (East & West).

What mattered: scriptoria, libraries, pilgrimage routes; vows that stabilized identity; endowments that stabilized operations.

Influence move: Preserve archives, law, and scientific fragments; become the quietly indispensable custodians of legitimacy, charity, diplomacy, and land.

Court Astrologers & Learned Physicians (Imperial/Caliphal courts).

What mattered: access to rulers; mathematical astronomy; pharmacology; discreet advisory functions.

Influence move: Translate technical skill into proximity; proximity into policy.

Esoteric Theological Circles.

What mattered: commentaries and catechetical chains with "outer" and "inner" readings.

Influence move: Gate advanced doctrine for those tasked with teaching or ruling; turn vocabulary into a filter for high office.

✓ High Medieval & Early Modern (c. 1100–1700)

Militarized Orders and Confraternities.

What mattered: vows, land, banking-like functions, and legal privileges; in cities, lay confraternities blend piety with mutual aid and lobbying.

Influence move: Professionalize logistics—pilgrimage, charity, finance—under sacred cover; become a backbone for trade and war.

Craft Guilds & Proto-Lodge Culture.

What mattered: oaths, graded skill ranks, ritualized admissions; meeting halls that doubled as courts of credit and reputation.

Influence move: Turn shop floors into schools of trust; convert trust into local sovereignty.

Occult-Philosophical Societies (Renaissance → Scientific Revolution).

What mattered: "invisible colleges," coded emblems, selective correspondence, cabinet laboratories.

Influence move: Protect experimental work in small circles; translate findings into patronage and statecraft when safe.

✓ Enlightenment & Nation-Forming Era (c. 1700–1900)

Fraternities and Learned Societies.

What mattered: constitutions, degrees, traveling warrants, standardized rituals; salons and clubs as recruitment funnels for administration, commerce, and reform.

Influence move: Manufacture cross-class, cross-regional elite cohesion; move petitions and appointments through private dining rooms faster than parliaments can.

Revolutionary Cells & Counter-Societies.

What mattered: clandestine printing, correspondence networks, safe houses; ritual to shape solidarity under duress.

Influence move: Use secrecy to synchronize action; use ritual to ensure loyalty; pivot from conspiracy to governance post-victory.

Private Banking & Discreet Trusts.

What mattered: quiet rooms where capital, law, and reputation meet; family houses stabilizing transnational credit.

Influence move: Turn discretion into a service; turn service into political veto power.

✓ Twentieth Century to Today (c. 1900–present)

Continuity-of-Government & Security Sanctuaries.

What mattered: hardened sites, deniable facilities, crisis scripts, and classification regimes; "licensed secrecy" under oversight (ideally). **Influence move:** Claim emergency legitimacy; professionalize secrecy with audits and warrants when pressured.

Elite Student Societies & Leadership Pipelines.

What mattered: early bonding, curated archives and traditions, alumni networks spanning finance, law, intelligence, and politics.

Influence move: Convert youthful belonging into life-long first-name access; make the dining room the real interview.

Global Forums & Offsite Conclaves.

What mattered: invitation lists, Chatham House rules, discreet side meetings.

Influence move: Align policy narratives across sectors pre-announcement; synchronize capital and regulation while maintaining plausible deniability.

Digital Orders (proto-forms).

What matters now: encrypted channels, invite-only communities, private models and datasets; algorithmic "switchboards."

Influence move: Migrate sanctuary and ritual into software; gate access by keys, compute, and social graph rather than stone thresholds.

Symbol Decoder: Emblems That Travel

Treat this section like a field guide. Symbols rarely "prove" membership; they *signal* continuity, aspiration, or inherited legitimacy. Decode them in context: stone, seal, minute book, badge, floor plan, oath.

Use rule: A symbol means what the *institutional context* lets it mean. Check the room, the ritual, the roster, and the dates.

A. Governance & Sovereignty

Double-Headed Eagle.

Signal: Sovereignty watching two domains (east/west; sacred/secular). Imperial or "universal" claims.

Field cues: Crowns, orbs, scepters; appear on charters, regalia, or in stone over main gates.

Investigator's note: When this appears in a private hall, ask what "two domains" its members believe they bridge (church/state; old money/new money; national/transnational).

Keys (Crossed).

Signal: Custody—of doctrine, archives, or gates. "We hold the binding and loosing power."

Field cues: Thresholds, chests, lock motifs; often paired with seals or oaths.

Move: Look for who controls admissions, who stamps minutes, and who keeps the archives.

Fasces (Bundle & Axe).

Signal: Authority by union—many bound into one.

Field cues: Courtrooms, assemblies, coinage.

Move: If this appears in private spaces, expect a group that prides itself on discipline and centralized enforcement.

B. Work & Virtue

Bee / Beehive.

Signal: Industry, order, collective production of sweetness (public good).

Field cues: Charity halls, guild crests, private banks emphasizing 'stability.'

Move: Examine actual deliverables (loans, scholarships, public works) to see if the symbol is earned or decorative.

Compass & Square / Plumb.

Signal: Measure and rectify; moral geometry; building and character.

Field cues: Lodge spaces, architects' halls, and scientific societies that inherited craft metaphors.

Move: Read the room's plan: sightlines, raised platforms, north-south axes. The architecture will mirror the ethic.

Anvil & Hammer / Trowel.

Signal: Craft, foundation-laying, practical virtue.

Field cues: Ceremony floors with checker patterns, cornerstones with dates, feature walls with tools.

Move: Trace the endowment that funds these rooms; it often hides a local switchboard of contracts and careers.

C. Mortality & Oath

Skull & Bones / Memento Mori.

Signal: Death-awareness, oath seriousness, rebirth into a new identity.

Field cues: Cellars, vault-like rooms, coffin props in degrees; candles and black drape.

Move: The rite is designed to imprint memory. Interview initiates (when ethical) about *how* the room felt, not just what was said.

Blazing Star / Radiant Eye (Within Triangle).

Signal: Watchfulness; inner light; providence or conscience above the human.

Field cues: Ceilings, dais backdrops, seals.

Move: Separate theology from pedagogy: Is the eye meant as divine surveillance or as a metaphor for cultivated attention?

D. Animals & Mythic Figures

Lion / Griffin.

Signal: Guardianship, strength, hybrid custody of domains (griffin = land/sky).

Field cues: Gateposts, archive doors, bank halls.

Move: Ask: What do these guardians guard—money, records, doctrine, reputation?

Serpent (Coiled or Ouroboros).

Signal: Cycles, knowledge, boundary policing (a snake marks a perimeter).

Field cues: Threshold tiles, ritual jewelry, diagrams.

Move: If the serpent eats its tail, look for doctrines of recurrence and renewal tied to organizational memory.

E. Numbers & Geometry

Three / Triangle.

Signal: Tripartite structures (place/symbol/script; body/soul/spirit; sanctuary/assembly/outer world).

Move: Many groups govern via triads: three officers, three veils, three knocks. Map real decision-making to the triad.

Seven / Heptagon / Seven Stars.

Signal: Completeness; planetary or grade systems; staged ascent.

Move: If seven grades exist, ask what competencies are added at each rung. Grades without competencies are theater.

Architecture as a Codebook

Buildings teach. The plan tells you what the group values; thresholds tell you who belongs; materials tell you what must endure. Learn to read four things quickly.

Thresholds & Axes

- **Processional lines.** Long, straight approaches build gravity; zig-zags slow and sort.

- **Sightlines.** What can everyone see? What is reserved for the inner ring?

- **Vertical moves.** Steps, platforms, and galleries create rank by elevation.

Materials & Acoustics

- **Stone = permanence** (archives, doctrine).

- **Wood = flexibility** (dining, negotiation).

- **Soft walls = secrecy** (sound-dampened deliberation).

- **Vaults = gravity** (memory and oath work).

Furniture & Props

- **Tables:** round (equality theater), long (ranked seating), horseshoe (leadership focal point).

- **Chairs:** raised chairs broadcast jurisdiction; matching chairs broadcast fraternity.

- **Chests & cabinets:** control of minutes, regalia, charters. Find the key holder.

Move: Sketch the seating chart after a meeting. Seat maps often outlive minutes in telling you who matters.

Hidden Infrastructure

- **Back stairs and service corridors** = deniable meetings and safe exits.

- **Safe rooms & "priest holes."** Micro-architecture of survival.

- **Signal hardware** (bells, lights) = choreography cues.

Ritual Anatomy: The Repeatable Script

Strip ritual to its mechanics. Most durable initiatory or decision-making rites follow this arc:

1. **Gate:** Candidate is separated (silence, hoodwink, fasting, cleansing).

2. **Ordeal:** Challenge or test (recitation, endurance, courage, composure).

3. **Disclosure:** Emblem or phrase revealed; narrative reframed.

4. **Charge:** Duties imposed; boundaries set; penalties (symbolic or explicit).

5. **Seal:** Shared meal or sign; entry in a register; token issued.

Investigative Protocols: Research Checklist (Disinformation-Proof)

Keep this checklist on the inside cover of your notebook. It keeps you from chasing ghosts, and it keeps your findings clean.

Step 1: Frame the Claim

- Write the claim as a single, testable sentence with a **time window** and **actors**.

  Example: "By 1984, Group X controlled the Y committee through Z alumni."

- Extract **keywords** (names, dates, places, emblems) and **adjacent terms** (front organizations, family names, codename projects).

Step 2: Map Sources (Primary → Secondary → Tertiary)

- **Primary:** Charters, minute books, rolls, ledgers, court records, property filings, FOIA/FOI releases, corporate registries, building permits, travel itineraries, endowments, wills, deed transfers, calendar notices.

- **Secondary:** Monographs, journal articles, credible histories, serious investigative reporting.

- **Tertiary:** Encyclopedias, crowd-edited summaries—good for orientation, never for proof.

Step 3: Cross-Check with the Four Lenses

1. **Money:** Bankers, trusts, endowments, payments, property.

2. **Meetings:** Rooms, guest lists, travel logs, calendar overlaps.

3. **Messaging:** Mottos, speeches, memos, emblems.

4. **Machinery:** Buildings, corridors, secure lines, procurement.

Illustration prompt: "Quadrant diagram—Money / Meetings / Messaging / Machinery—sample evidence types listed in each."

Step 4: Architecture Walkthrough

- Sketch the **plan** (doors, dais, galleries).

- Mark **thresholds** (who can pass).

- Note **acoustics** (private/public).

- Photograph discreetly where legal; never trespass.

Step 5: People Graph

- Build a **bipartite graph**: people ↔ institutions (boards, trusts, lodges, clubs, committees).

- Track **temporal edges** (start/end years).

- Highlight **bridge figures** (the two-club banker, the judge on the charity board, the rector with a financial post).

Step 6: Date Discipline

- Use **absolute dates** ("21 March 1984"), not "spring 1984," whenever possible.

- When a story says "recently," replace it with the actual date.

- Align dates with **ritual calendars** (feasts, commencements, anniversaries) to see why a meeting was timed the way it was.

Step 7: Disinformation Filters

- **Noise inflation:** Wild claims appear immediately after credible disclosures. Split the two.

- **Brand hijack:** Popular emblems attached to unrelated groups to bait you. Confirm provenance.

- **Mirror networks:** Adversarial factions adopt similar secrecy— don't confuse reflection for coordination.

Step 8: Ethics & Safety

- Protect living sources; never publish personal data that invites harassment.

- Keep records so your work is auditable.

- Know local law (photography, archives, defamation).

- Don't over-promise; publish what you can show.

Reflection Prompts: Which Patterns Resonate Today?

Use these prompts to test your understanding against the present. The value is in the specifics you write down.

1. **Capability:** What capability today (compute, payments, identity, logistics, messaging) is becoming the new sanctuary? Who controls it?

_____

_____

_____

_____

_____

_____

_____

2. **Calendar:** Which recurring dates (summits, offsites, convocations, retreats) seem to precede major policy shifts or market moves in your country?

_____

_____

_____

_____

_____

_____

_____

_____

3. **Switchboard:** Who are the three cross-sector "bridge" figures
   you see most often? What rooms do they sit in, and what
   outcomes move through them?

_____

_____

_____

_____

_____

_____

4. **Exit Costs:** Where do you see high exit costs locking talent
   inside legacy networks? What alternative ladders could reduce
   those costs?

_____

_____

_____

_____

_____

_____

_____

_____

5. **Sanctuary Ethics:** Which sanctuaries deserve protection (journalism, research labs, dissident shelters), and which sanctuaries demand public rules (payments, public-impact deliberations)? Draw the line.

_____

_____

_____

_____

_____

_____

_____

6. **Symbol Literacy:** Which three emblems recur most in the institutions that shape your life? How is each one *used* (room + ritual + record + roster + date)?

_____

_____

_____

_____

_____

_____

_____

_____

7. **Architecture:** Map one building where decisions get made. Where are the thresholds, the back stairs, the "waiting rooms"? How do those features shape who speaks and who decides?

_____

_____

_____

_____

_____

_____

8. **Ritual:** Identify one modern rite (onboarding, oath, swearing-in, fellowship dinner). What are its Gate, Ordeal, Disclosure, Charge, and Seal?

_____

_____

_____

_____

_____

_____

_____

_____

9. **Continuity:** Which family names, endowments, or trusts appear across decades? What do they fund? Who do they place?

_____

_____

_____

_____

_____

_____

_____

_____

10. **Your Role:** Which rooms should *you* be in? Which should you avoid? What skill can you build that lets you enter new rooms on honest terms?

_____

_____

_____

_____

_____

_____

_____

_____

Applied Exercises

These are hands-on drills you can run in an afternoon or over a week. They convert reading into a skill.

Exercise A: The "Room Read" (90 minutes)

1. Pick a public building where decisions are made (council chamber, courthouse, boardroom used for hearings).

2. Sketch the plan from memory after a short visit or virtual tour: doors, dais, galleries, alcoves.

3. Mark: where people wait, where private conversations can occur unheard, where staff can enter unseen.

4. Write 200 words on how the room's plan biases outcomes.

_____

_____

_____

_____

_____

_____

_____

_____

_____

_____

_____

_____

_____

_____

_____

_____

Exercise B: Symbol–Context Match (2 hours)

1. Photograph (legally) or collect images of five emblems in your city.

2. For each, fill the matrix: Room • Ritual • Record • Roster • Date.

3. Write a short paragraph on how the symbol's meaning changes across contexts.

_____

_____

_____

_____

_____

_____

_____

_____

_____

_____

_____

_____

_____

_____

_____

_____

_____

_____

_____

_____

_____

_____

Exercise C: Calendar Overlay (Half-day)

1. Build a calendar of your city's/domains' recurring gatherings (convocations, trade association meetings, fiscal events).

2. Overlay notable announcements from the past three years.

3. Highlight clusters.

4. Draft a hypothesis: "Announcements of type X follow event Y by Z days because…"

_____

_____

_____

_____

_____

_____

_____

_____

_____

_____

_____

_____

_____

_____

_____

_____

_____

_____

_____

_____

_____

_____

_____

Exercise D: People Graph (One week)

1. Choose one "bridge figure."

2. Chart their public affiliations year-by-year for 15 years.

3. Identify the three rooms where their presence coincides with outcomes (funding decisions, hires, regulations).

4. Write a neutral profile focusing on capability and coordination, not gossip.

_____

_____

_____

_____

_____

_____

_____

_____

_____

9) Case Mapping Templates

Use these one-page templates repeatedly. They're designed to keep your analysis tight.

Template 1: Order / Site Overview

- Name (current/historical): _____

- Location(s): _____

- Sanctuary (place + access control): _____

- Capability (what is being preserved/coordinated):
  _____

- Ritual (gate/ordeal/disclosure/charge/seal):
  _____

- Switchboard (who talks to whom, through what channel):
  _____

- Continuity (endowments, archives, legal shells): _____

- Public interface (licensed? tolerated? deniable?): _____

- Exit costs (low/medium/high + why): _____

- Primary traces located: _____

Template 2: Meeting Readout

- Date / Time / Place: _____

- Occasion (cover story vs actual agenda if known): _____

- Attendees (roles, not gossip): _____

- Seating plan/speaking order: _____

- Decisions / Assignments observed: _____

- Follow-ups (who meets where next): _____

- Artifacts (documents, props, emblems): _____

Template 3: Symbol Use Report

- Symbol & form (stone, print, seal, textile): _____

- First appearance (date/source): _____

- Context (room/ritual/record/roster/date): _____

- Competing interpretations (list, with evidence):

_____

_____

_____

_____

_____

- Your assessment (most likely meaning in this context):

_____

_____

_____

_____

_____

_____

_____

_____

_____

_____

_____

_____

_____

_____

_____

_____

_____

_____

_____

_____

_____

_____

_____

Resource Library: Archives, Declassified Files & Research Aids

You asked for practical sources without fluff. Here's a curated list of **repositories and tools** (not personalities) that help you trace capability, sanctuary, continuity, and switchboards. Always respect local law, archiving rules, and privacy.

Government & Intergovernmental Archives

- **National Archives (multiple countries).** Deeds, wills, charters, cabinet papers, war files, and intelligence releases. Search finding aids by **family names, trusts, lodges, companies, and building addresses.**

- **Parliamentary & Congressional Archives.** Committee minutes, witness lists, member interests, travel disclosures.

- **Municipal Archives & Land Registries.** Building permits, ownership chains, heritage reports (often rich in architectural detail).

- **Courts & Gazettes.** Company strikes off, charity registrations, bankruptcy filings, official notices; read the fine print.

- **International Organizations.** UN, Council of Europe, EU, etc.—treaty drafting histories, conference rosters, observer accreditation

Declassified & Freedom-of-Information Gates

- **FOIA/FOI Portals.** File politely; specify dates, offices, and keywords; ask for **indices** and **finding aids** when records are denied.

- **Declassification Reading Rooms.** Digitized collections of previously secret cables, memos, and reports—searchable by topic, date, and office.

- **National Security & Diplomatic Document Projects (university-hosted).** Curated dossiers with context notes; good for triangulating dates and actors.

Corporate & Financial Trails

- **Company Registries.** Directors, secretaries, beneficial owners (jurisdiction-dependent), charge filings.

- **Securities Filings.** Executive bios, related-party transactions, governance structures.

- **Procurement Databases.** Who gets contracts for security, archives, ritual regalia (!), or meeting venues; look for clustering of vendors across agencies.

- **Charity Regulators.** Trustees, annual accounts, restricted funds, and grantmaking patterns.

Built Environment & Maps

- **Historic Environment Records / National Monuments Databases.** Plans, elevations, and significance statements often include **phased** construction notes that reveal when hidden rooms were added.

- **Sanborn-type Fire Insurance Maps / Ordnance Survey archives.** Footprints, building materials, internal divisions— clues to hidden corridors and vaults.

- **Zoning & Planning Portals.** Meeting minutes, objections, lawyer letters; a goldmine for "who really cares" about a site.

Libraries & Digital Collections

- **University Special Collections.** Minutes of clubs, fraternities, and learned societies; alumni magazines; donor plaques you can match to archives.

- **Digitized Pamphlets & Ephemera.** Small-run tracts, invitations, programs—often the only printed traces of certain rites or meetings.

- **Newspapers & Trade Journals.** Obituaries (life summaries reveal affiliations), society pages (dinners, balls), legal notices.

OSINT & Cross-Checking Tools

- **Flight / Vessel Trackers.** Tie private meetings to travel patterns.

- **Domain & Corporate Graph Tools.** Track who owns the website for a "trust," who shares addresses, and who shares counsel.

- **Open Tender Monitors.** Which venue gets booked repeatedly for "strategic retreats"?

- **Genealogy Databases.** Old money often equals old memberships. Treat sensitively; avoid doxxing.

Timeline Worksheets (Fill-In)

Use these blank frameworks to build **your** localized timeline without drowning in detail.

Worksheet A: Local Orders & Sites (Century Bands)

- 1100s:

  Sites   /   Orders   /   Capabilities:
  _____

- 1200s:

  Sites   /   Orders   /   Capabilities:
  _____

- 1300s:

  Sites   /   Orders   /   Capabilities:
  _____

- 1400s:

  _____

  Sites   /   Orders   /   Capabilities:

  _____

Worksheet B: Continuity Map

- Endowment   /   Trust   Name:

  _____

- Founder   &   Successors:

  _____

- Assets (property, archives, cash): _____

- Beneficiaries:

  _____

- Boards   &   Overlaps:

  _____

- Ritual   /   Calendar   Links:

  _____

- Public Interface (licensed/tolerated/deniable): _____

_____

_____

_____

_____

_____

_____

Symbol–Ritual–Outcome Case Studies (Mini-Guides)

These mini-guides help you practice *connecting* an emblem or rite to an outcome rather than treating it as independent décor.

Case 1: Laurel & Threshold

- **Symbol in Room:** Laurel crown carved over the inner doorway.

- **Ritual Observed:** New members processed through this door after a charge.

- **Outcome Pattern:** Entrants disproportionately placed on **selection committees** within one year.

- **Hypothesis:** The threshold ritual marks a pool from which gatekeepers are drawn; laurel ≈ "license to judge."

- **Evidence to Seek:** Appointment letters; committee rosters; minutes of votes; alumni notes praising "judgment" or "taste."

Case 2: Keys & Charter Chest

- **Symbol in Room:** Crossed keys on a heavy chest in the corner.

- **Ritual Observed:** Minutes and regalia are locked away immediately after meetings.

- **Outcome Pattern:** Information asymmetry; non-key holders rely on rumor, key holders control narratives.

- **Hypothesis:** Custody of the keys ≈ is custody of institutional memory.

- **Evidence to Seek:** Who holds keys? How are minutes approved? How does access correlate with promotions?

Case 3: Vault & Memento Mori

- **Symbol in Room:** Skull on a lectern; coffin prop along the wall.

- **Ritual Observed:** "Death to old self" oath with low-light reveal.

- **Outcome Pattern:** High retention; strong favor trading; low whistleblowing.

- **Hypothesis:** The rite imprints loyalty and silence; breaking it would feel like a social death.

- **Evidence to Seek:** Exit patterns; off-cycle promotions; disciplinary records (if any); alumni who leave—why, how, consequences.

Pattern Library: Phrases that Signal the Operating System

You'll hear certain phrases in minutes, speeches, and toasts. They're not throwaway lines; they're operating hints.

- **"Fit and proper."** Gatekeeping code—moral geometry checks.

- **"Councils of peace."** Off-calendar, off-record meetings framed as reconciliation or strategy.

- **"The family."** It may mean a literal dynasty or a metaphor for a cross-sector network.

- **"By ancient usage."** Procedural veto against reform without debate.

- **"For want of a better room."** A move to relocate a decision to a sanctuary.

Building Your Own Code of Practice

You'll do better work—and avoid becoming part of someone else's theater—if you decide, now, how you'll conduct yourself.

1. **No trespass.** If you can't legally enter, you don't.

2. **No secret recordings in private homes or spiritual sanctuaries.** Ethics first.

3. **Anonymize civilians.** Punch up, not down.

4. **Proportionality.** Report what is *material* to public outcomes, not private peccadillos.

5. **Right of reply.** Before publishing about living persons, summarize your claims to them and offer a short window for factual correction.

Quick-Reference: Red Flags vs. Green Flags

This page is a cheat sheet. Pin it by your desk.

Red Flags (leverage over shelter):

- No minutes, ever, for decisions affecting the public.

- Exit costs are punitive (career, legal, social).

- Rituals designed to humiliate or extract—not to bind to service.

- Symbols used to demand obedience rather than to teach duty.

- Ownership and funding chains vanish into nominees and shells with no service rationale.

Green Flags (shelter over leverage):

- Time-boxed secrecy with audits and scheduled declassification.

- Low exit costs; alumni thrive without insider patronage.

- Rituals teach duty, courage, craft—not silence for silence's sake.

- Symbols explained to members as *values*, not threats.

- Funding/endowment reports show consistent public-interest outputs.

Long-Form Questions

These are the big ones. Take your time. The value is in the specifics you record.

Q1. Name one "hidden order" in your city that likely *deserves* protection (shelter for dissent, investigative journalism, medical R&D). What rules should govern its secrecy?

_____

_____

_____

_____

_____

_____

_____

_____

_____

_____

_____

_____

_____

_____

_____

_____

_____

_____

_____

_____

_____

_____

Q2. Name one "hidden order" that likely *demands* accountability (payments, identity, crisis comms). What rules and audits should bind it?

_____

_____

Q3. Map a policy outcome you care about from the announcement back to rooms. Where was it rehearsed? Who carried drafts between rooms? What rituals bonded the coalition?

_____

_____

_____

_____

_____

_____

_____

Q4. Which symbol have you misread in the past? Redecode it with the context matrix (room/ritual/record/roster/date).

_____

_____

_____

_____

_____

_____

_____

_____

_____

_____

_____

_____

_____

_____

_____

_____

_____

_____

_____

_____

_____

_____

Q5. If you were to found a **pro-social sanctuary** tomorrow, what would be its capability, its guardrails, and its graduation ritual?

_____

_____

Final Word

This workbook is meant to make you effective, not paranoid. The patterns we've studied—sanctuary, ritual, continuity, switchboards, calendars—are human constants. Sometimes they shelter what is precious. Sometimes they shelter what preys. Literacy is the difference between the two outcomes.

You now have a working method, a field kit, and the discipline to use both. Keep going. Update your maps. Share what you can show. Protect what must be sheltered. And never forget the core rule: when a room sets public outcomes, it must accept public rules.

Conclusion

Let's bring the threads together without pretending the work is "done." You asked for a sober, operational view of hidden orders—how secrecy, ritual, and continuity shape decisions that later show up as inevitabilities in textbooks. You asked for a way to read power in two layers at once: the theater and the choreography behind it. You've got it now—a lens rather than a single theory—and this conclusion is about turning that lens into durable habits.

You've seen the recurring machinery: sanctuaries where coordination can survive pressure, symbols that compress identity, scripts that imprint loyalty, switchboards that route favors and decisions, and stories that justify all four. You've also seen the other side: how those same mechanisms, when bounded by rules and oriented to service, preserve fragile knowledge, protect dissent, and help communities ride out shocks. There are no pantomime villains or saints in this terrain. There are rooms, procedures, calendars, and outcomes—some pro-social, some extractive, many mixed. The task is to tell the difference, act accordingly, and build better rooms where we can.

What the Investigation Established

First, history has two speeds. One is the public cadence—elections, rulings, speeches, wars. The other is the private cadence—off-calendar retreats, minute books no one sees, initiation nights, dinner circuits, and the long half-life of endowments and trusts. When you put the two clocks side by side, events that once looked random start to make sense. That is literacy, not paranoia. It is the discipline of asking "which room" and "which ritual calendar" sit behind a headline that insists it "just happened."

Second, capability beats scandal. Exposés clear fog; they rarely dismantle useful infrastructure. A sanctuary that houses crisis coordination or financial plumbing will survive disclosure if it keeps working. That is why naming and shaming, by itself, disappoints. Durable reform either reduces monopoly power (plural centers) or lowers the cost of exit (rival pipelines). Anything else is theater from the other side.

Third, the ethical line is concrete. Secrecy as shelter is one thing: protecting investigative work, endangered memory, patient data, dissident safety. Secrecy as leverage is another: laundering reputations, extracting rents, staging "consensus" in ways that sidestep consent. The test is simple: **what does the secrecy enable in the world?** If it consistently protects capabilities that the public needs and submits to time-boxed oversight, it's licensed. If it consistently shapes public outcomes without rules, it's private sovereignty.

The Patterns, Restated Plainly

Across the eras in this book, the same moves repeat.

- **Ancient temples, omen guilds, and mysteries** used oaths, thresholds, and calendars to gate potent knowledge. They protected competence (calendrics, medicine, ethics) with a ritual that made memory stick.

- **Medieval orders, guilds, and monasteries** fused service with sovereignty: logistics and learning under vows. The meeting hall, scriptorium, and vault were policy in wood and stone.

- **Early modern fraternities, salons, and private banks** professionalized discretion and standardized belonging. They manufactured trust at scale, then translated it into appointments, credit, and reforms—sometimes enlightened, often self-serving.

- **Contemporary sanctuaries**—from leadership pipelines and private forums to continuity-of-government sites and deniable facilities—moved the same functions into new materials: glass, steel, encryption. The pitches changed; the mechanics did not.

You can dislike some of this, but you can't wish it away. Humans will keep building rooms; the future is a question of **which** rooms, **how many**, **under what rules**, and **with what exits**.

Why the Myths Persist (and What to Do With Them)

Myths glue people to causes and make hard asks tolerable. Initiations feel real because they compress pain, story, and sensory cues into a single, once-in-a-lifetime moment. Symbols recur because they compress continuity—'we were here before you were born'—into a small piece of visual grammar. Stories of ancient pedigrees and "hidden masters" persist because they give elites a pedigree and aspirants a map. None of that is an automatic indictment; it becomes one when myth shields incompetence or abuse.

Your protocol going forward looks like this:

- **Disentangle romance from function.** Ritual might be beautiful; judge it by what it builds and guards.

- **Expect adaptation.** Orders mutate under scrutiny—names change, shells are swapped, rooms move. Track functions, not labels.

- **Use dates relentlessly.** Replace "recently" with calendar dates. Align key decisions with recurring gatherings and anniversaries; you'll see the cadence behind the script.

From Literacy to Agency

A map that only entertains is a waste. Here's how to convert literacy into action without turning into a scold or a cynic.

For individuals: Diversify affiliations so no single switchboard can price your integrity. Keep quiet records of commitments made and delivered; never rely on vibes where a dated note will do. Learn a concrete skill (legal, financial, technical) that travels across rooms; capability dethrones gatekeeping.

For organizations: Build sanctuaries with guardrails—renewable secrecy warrants, rotating auditors from distinct institutions, and after-action disclosures written in plain language. If you need privacy to deliver public goods, ask for it explicitly and show your homework afterward.

For civic life: Make exit cheaper. Scholarships, open fellowships, interoperable credentials, transparent procurement, and simple, public recruitment paths—each of these erodes private monopolies the way water wears stone. Expose abuses, yes; but also **substitute**: new ladders beat old ladders, moralizing at them.

For researchers and journalists: Don't frame everything as a plot. Show the workflow: room → ritual → roster → record → outcome. When you can't show it, say so. When you can, cite two independent traces and let readers check your work. That's how you keep the field clean and keep disinformation from hitching a ride.

The Future Rooms (and How Not to Fear Them)

The next sanctuaries are less stone and more compute. Expect:

- **Algorithmic switchboards.** Decision-weighted social graphs and private models routing capital, hiring, and narrative at a speed no steering committee can match. The emblem is not a crest but an API key.

- **Hybrid sanctuaries.** Physical rooms mirrored by digital shadows: a secure deliberation now, an auto-published "decision dossier" later; a private archive now, a scheduled release.

- **Crisis federalism.** Cascading failures (supply chain, grid, information) will license new rooms to claim emergency mandates. The safeguard is federation: many rooms, standard interfaces, no single sovereign cloister deciding for everyone.

Don't panic; specify. Ask the five questions. Demand the single rule. Design rooms that can be private **and** bounded, decisive **and** reviewed, fast **and** accountable. Rituals are not going away; use them to teach duty, courage, and craft rather than obedience for its own sake.

What We Choose Next

The choice in front of us is not "secrets or no secrets." It's whether a small set of rooms will harden into private sovereignties, or whether we will insist on a world with many rooms, many routes, and rules that reach them all. That choice unfolds in mundane places: planning committees that decide whether a lab must file declassification schedules; fellowship boards that decide whether to open applications; regulators who decide when discretion protects the public and when it needs a leash; designers who decide whether the building plan has a back stair that only the powerful can use.

This book has tried to do three simple things so you can be decisive in those moments:

1. **Name the machinery**—sanctuary, symbol, script, switchboard, story—so you can recognize it without mystique.

2. **Show the workflow**—gate, ordeal, disclosure, charge, seal—so you can tell when a rite is building competence or laundering control.

3. **Give you a rule**—public outcomes, public rules—so you can hold a line without endless arguments about motive.

None of that requires you to become a professional archivist or a full-time critic. It asks you to become a competent citizen of a complicated world: someone who can step into a room, notice the thresholds and the seating plan, sense the ritual arc, map the switchboard, and ask for the right guardrails with a straight face and a steady voice. It asks you to build rooms that deserve loyalty and to leave rooms that don't—without drama, without flinching, without two minds about what fairness demands.

A Last Word to the Reader

If you remember nothing else, remember this: most "hidden" orders are not mysterious when someone finally shows you the room. They're familiar human trades—logistics, law, finance, archives, succession—surrounded by choreography that manufactures belonging and authority. The danger isn't that such rooms exist; the danger is when we let them become **unreviewable** while they set the conditions of life for everyone else.

You have one task now: use your literacy. When you walk past a crest, ask where else it appears. When you see a vaulted door, ask what's stored and who holds the key. When a policy appears "from nowhere," ask which calendar it rhymes with. When you're invited into a room, notice the thresholds and the exits before you admire the table. When the moment comes to build or fund a room, insist on the rule. And if the room refuses, build another—and make it better.

This is not a crusade. It is a craft. And craft scales. If enough people adopt it—in councils, labs, newsrooms, courts, companies, universities, congregations—hidden orders will still exist, but fewer of them will be able to decide our fate without our informed consent.

That is the adult settlement for a complex century: rooms that do hard things, rituals that build character, continuities that preserve what matters, and oversight that keeps every one of those assets in its proper place. If the investigation you've just completed gives you the language and the confidence to ask for that—and to build it where you can—then the book has done its job.

www.ingramcontent.com/pod-product-compliance
Lightning Source LLC
Chambersburg PA
CBHW060736050426
42449CB00008B/1249